SHATTERED AMERICAN DREAM

N. Anta Gueye-James

ISBN: 979-8-9897876-2-3

Publisher: Winn Publications, Melbourne, Fl | winnpublications.com
Cover Design: N. Anta Gueye James, Kraftsxalil of RBS Crew, Arilia Winn
Cover Illustrator: Kraftsxalil of RBS Crew, Arilia Winn
Editors: Kirsten Rees | Book Editor & Author Coach
CaTyra Polland | Editor at Love for Words
Foreword: Sharon Hurley Hall

Connect with the author:

LinkedIn (LinkedIn.com/in/decolonizer)
Twitter (X) @rbldecolonizer
Instagram (@rebeldecolonizer)
Threads (@rebeldecolonizer)
Website: www.rebeldecolonizer.com

Acknowledgments

Thank you, Claudia and Gnima, for your feedback and time. Thank you, Sharon, for your support and foreword, you saw me and that means so much.

I dedicate this book to my late mother, the always fierce supporter of her children in her actions and fervent prayers for us. I wish you were still here because we were not done making you happy on earth, but I am convinced you watch over us from above because I can still feel the magnitude and effect of your prayers daily. You will forever be my angel mom. I love and miss you.

Table of Contents

Foreword

Preface

SAD 1: **The Lure**   pg. 1
Falling in love with America

SAD 2: **The Pull**   pg. 13
Shooting down red flags for the sake of love

SAD 3: **The Fight for America**   pg. 25
You shall not stand between me and my love

SAD 4: **Coming to America**   pg. 45
When the eaglet first landed

SAD 5: **From Petty to Wise**   pg. 61
Discovering the seeds of white supremacy

SAD 6: **Learning Service**   pg. 71
The beautiful nuggets

SAD 7: **Becoming a Number**   pg. 79
Renamed then redefined by a social security number, a credit score, and sometimes a whole new life story

SAD 8: **The *System* and the *Man* are real**   pg. 89
Discovering the true face of America

SAD 9: **THUG LIFE**   pg. 103
Breaking up with America and extracting my child
from her birthplace

Dear United States of America   pg. 109

Reflection Questions   pg. 111

About the Author   pg. 114

Works Cited   pg. 116

Foreword - An Illusion Unmasked

By Sharon Hurley Hall, author of *I'm Tired of Racism: True Stories of Existing While Black*

We've been living through unprecedented times, yet they often feel all too 'precedented' – and certainly predictable. As the heat goes out of many racial justice initiatives, folx pull back on DEI commitments, and there are active steps in the USA to send us back a couple of centuries in terms of rights for many deliberately disadvantaged groups, N Anta Gueye's autobiographical book, *Shattered American Dream* unmasks the disconnect between the public persona of the USA and the reality Black and Global Majority people experience when living there.

The full circle journey of Anta's love affair with the USA and how and why that ended will resonate with many people who are considering a 'Blaxit' – leaving the USA in search of a country which is more hospitable to Black people in the ways that truly matter – with little or no racism, equal access to necessary services, and true opportunity.

Anta's journey certainly resonated with me. As someone who grew up in a post-colonial environment – the Caribbean compared to Anta's Senegal – many of the perspectives and concerns she raised felt startlingly familiar despite the thousands of miles that separate our homes.

Why leave the Global North for the Global South? Because the country of her birth offered an enticing and much safer combination of invisibility and high expectations without the need for active shooter drills and the risk of either not making it to adulthood or being criminalized. Whatever the percentages, it's a valid fear for many Black parents.

As Anta charts the beginning and end of her love affair with the USA, there's a tension that informs and permeates the book, beautifully articulated in the prologue:

"By moving to the US, I went from being black (something I never had to individually think about daily) to BECOMING black (something I had to be mindful of every day)."

It's a shift many Black folx living and working in white-dominated spaces will relate to, whether they are in those spaces by birth or by immigration. And underlying that tension is an even older tension – between the knowledge that the success of the USA – and of many European countries – was built on the backs, literally, of enslaved Africans and their descendants, and the refusal to fully acknowledge or repair that harm. Indeed, as this book is released, many parts of the USA are actively trying to ensure that the full story of that particular genocide is never told.

As many of us know all too well, existing while Black in the USA, and in white-dominated spaces, is far from easy. As a Black person, you are at the mercy of daily slights and aggressions, invalidations, exclusions and more - and that's before we even consider the consistent reaping of Black lives by entitled white folx. No matter how you look at it, the words the country purports to live by are in no way matched by either systemic or interpersonal actions. Advocates, we see you, but right now it feels like a stalemate at best.

Shattered American Dream makes that clear. In nine impactful chapters, it tracks the journey from being enticed by the vision of the US to the realization that what it promises – opportunity and freedom – were not intended for anyone but white folx and removing herself and her family because of that realization.

Anta also reveals the dichotomy at the heart of typical media representations of the USA, which present white America as an ideal, while simultaneously showcasing a skewed view of Black experiences, as if deliberately intended to divide Black people in the country and diaspora from each other. As the author says, that's what white supremacy does, and you can see its workings through the stories and experiences she shares.

Throughout the book, Anta highlights a consistent thread of a deliberate policy of division. It's particularly clear as she experiences These divisions become even clearer when she gets to the US and highlights the resentments some African Americans feel towards Africans for "selling them into enslavement". It's an eye-opening section, though the author is clear where the ultimate responsibility lies. And I personally learned more about African resistance than we ever hear - a necessary addition to this story.

Shattered American Dream also gives significant insight into life in Senegal, from the family politics and relationships, the ideas about schooling and the emotional highs and lows the author experiences in trying to achieve her dream to the fact that even in a country where blackness doesn't need to be discussed, white supremacy can rule.

If the first third of the book provides the background to the author's USA experience, the next few chapters reveal the rotten underbelly of the myth of meritocracy, of moving from seeing people like yourself in every role -

something that resonated with me personally - to hardly seeing people like you represented at all. Readers will appreciate the value of a view from someone with a non-westernized educational background – it's a valuable perspective we don't often get and allows for plenty of myth busting. For example, she calls out the "starving children in Africa" trope while pointing out that there are, sadly, plenty of food insecure kids right there in the USA.

Throughout the book the disparity between the idea of America as the best country and how Black and Brown people are treated is revealed. Anta keeps highlighting things that just don't make sense – like the way some names are more difficult than others, and the systemic barriers to education, good health, decent housing and more. Black Americans know this viscerally, but the perspective of a relative outsider is valuable.

For me, the most poignant sentence in the book came with the author's "last straw" incident – the murder of Trayvon Martin, among a heartbreaking list of many other deaths. "Black lives did not seem to matter, and I was a Black life." In choosing the exit, and charting that exit, the author provides an insight into the decisions many Black people are facing now. Many of those who have the option to do so – for not everyone does – have chosen to raise our children outside the reach of the white gaze.

We know that any story told from the perspective of the colonizers and their descendants is partial at best, and deliberately disingenuous at worst. Anta's book starts to redress the balance by showing perspectives from a different educational tradition less influenced by white norms. As such, her indictment that "America only loves the white supremacist reflection of itself" is particularly damning.

By opening a window on the story of Black immigration to the USA from the perspective of a Black Muslim woman, and the author's subsequent choice to return to her country of birth, *Shattered American Dream* fills a gap many of us didn't realize was there. Black stories matter, and this is one that's not often told, which is why this is an important and necessary read.

<u>Disclaimer</u>

Events are described to the best of my recollection and with honesty and no ill-intention, only a commitment to share my lived experience in all its form in the hopes of raising awareness.

Preface - When the 'Land of Opportunity' is elsewhere, and you must leap.

In 2019, I wrote this farewell letter:

I can no longer say that this country, where I have lived longer than anywhere else in my life, where I became a naturalized citizen almost 10 years ago, where I poured sweat and tears as a productive member of society, is the land of freedom and opportunity. I cannot say that this is where I want to raise my child. I cannot guarantee that this USA will naturally support me as I teach my child the power of her blackness.

It will be a daily uphill battle to ensure she un-learns what society tells her and absorbs what I will spend countless hours injecting to build her up – something my parents never needed to consciously do because I grew up in [West Africa] a society that naturally made the power of my blackness a standard. I want her to grow up realizing her power before she, like I did when I moved here, understands the challenges it constitutes in certain environments…

I want her to own her inner power, beauty, and strength as the foundation upon which to handle these challenges. This is not to say she will not face other issues; she will, as I did growing up, but in the face of continued social injustice and glaringly overt racial inequity, bigotry, and racism, I am choosing those challenges as I move her – us – from America to Senegal, to Africa. I am ensuring that what she gains makes what she might lose worth letting go of. I want to prepare my child from a place where what I teach her is reinforced by what she sees around her, and I want to give her what I was given.

I want my child to know and feel that being like her mommy – an unapologetically black, foreign-born US citizen, voluntarily covered (!) Muslim woman – is A-OK! So, I am taking that leap. [July 2019]

I sent this farewell letter to my colleagues at the Washington Regional Association of Grantmakers' Racial Equity Working Group when I decided to leave the United States of America and move my family to West Africa. I emailed this letter then I found out at the very next group meeting just how much emotions and conversations these words had elicited in their own homes.

Like many African immigrants, I moved to the US as a young student, in the late nineties, with dreams of "Land of the Free, Home of the Brave". To the country where I could be whatever I wanted to be, where opportunity abounds and where everyone can make it. I held these views despite the fact that the first book I read in English was *The Autobiography of Malcolm X*.

I developed a rebellious, activist spirit very early in life, but when I read that book and layered it with the projection of America to the rest of the world through movies and entertainment, pop culture, their embassies' work, and their world leadership, I didn't suspect that the realities in this 1965 book were still painfully and systemically relevant. And so, I chose the USA.

In 23 years, I met great people, developed strong friendships, and learned an awful lot, especially about service. I challenged myself and my capabilities, forged my budding character to become the strong adult I am today. But there was a rude awakening to that journey: I discovered black as a race, a challenge, a determinant of life and health, a checkbox on every single form I needed to fill out. In moving to the US, I went from BEING black (something I never had to individually think about daily) to BECOMING black (something I had to be mindful of every day).

Through a career in health equity, I quickly uncovered a very different America than the one I grew up thinking I knew. Instead, I found a country with a foundation of white supremacy that never included black and brown people in "We the People", a system that wasn't built for non-whites to win. So yes, it WAS the land of opportunity, the land of the free, the country where you could be whatever you wanted to be... just not for people of color. America had lied to me, and I didn't want to lie to my daughter about it by singing along with her to some "I know I can be what I wanna be" if I truly didn't believe it.

Bringing my four-year-old to Senegal was the best decision I made for us: she is happy, fully bilingual, loves her hair, and has asked about the US only once as I write this. I watch her blossom and it warms my heart. I enrolled her in a bilingual school with lots of kids from all over the world, where she fits right in. So fast, in fact, that her teachers couldn't believe it.

My daughter sees people who look like her everywhere. When the president is announced, he looks like her; when she looks up at billboards, she sees people with her complexion and her hair texture. She isn't in a minority, she doesn't seem *different*... black is the standard, black is beautiful, black is normal. Nobody will revel at how 'articulate' she is in this environment because that's the norm and not an exception somehow unexpected from people of color.

I trust this move will give her the foundation to understand the power of her blackness. And so, when she goes out into the world, or decides one day to move back to her birth country, the United States of America, that power eclipses the challenge of her blackness. But by then, with what I am seeing as a possible turning point in racial equity today, she hopefully won't have to.

When I wrote the farewell letter to my colleagues, I knew it warranted more storytelling because it was a lot to unpack. It was published in Community Commons in 2020. I committed to one day doing the work of telling the story in more detail and sharing it with the world. I felt that my younger self would have liked to hear it and I feel like I owe it to today's youth to share it.

Our experiences are not meant for us alone.

And, as much as we can contribute to each other's journeys in ways that make sharing safe, we should enrich humanity with our experiences.

It took me years to complete this book. I had days of utter writer's block and days of completely unstoppable flow. I laughed, I cried, I reminisced...

but in no way did I ever regret a moment, no matter how hard or challenging to remember.

I am fully aware that every bit of this journey contributed to making me who I am today. And I love who I am: woman, black, African, Muslim, sister, daughter, friend, mother. An activist and supporter of everything black, an unapologetic daughter of the motherland, and defender of its interests. I am proud of the mix of culture in me and the diversity of thinking it has afforded me; I am proud to be Senegalese and I am proud to be American.

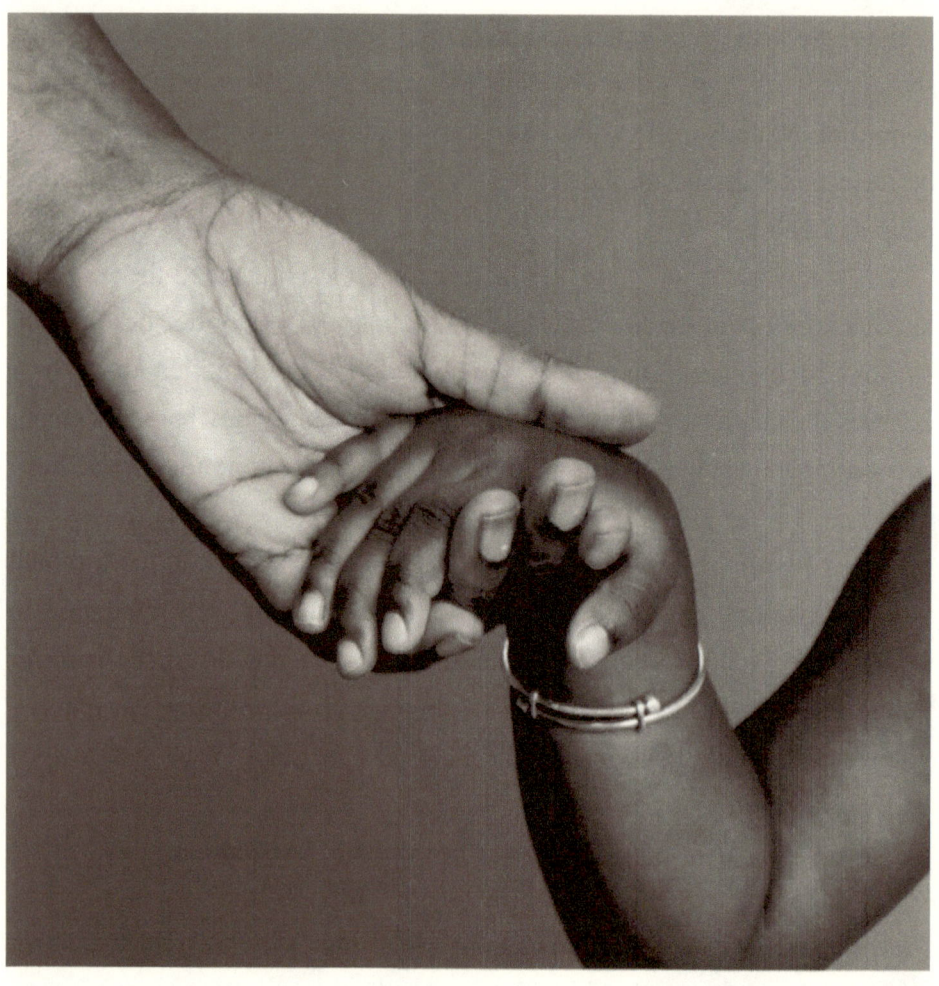

Picture of my hand holding my daughter's on her 3rd birthday in 2019, a few months before we left the US

SAD 1: The Lure

Falling in love with America

It must have been around 1 o'clock in the morning, on a school night, when my little brother shook me from my deep sleep with excitement. "It's on, it's on, let's go watch!"

The NBA: that's what was worth losing sleep over, risking big trouble if our parents realized we were up watching TV that late. But hey... it was the NBA!! Michael Jordan, Scottie Pippen, Isiah Thomas, and the Detroit Pistons bad boys... we were fa-sci-na-ted. Period! And by hell or high water, we were going to be watching these playoff games and be on point debating the American news at school for sure.

So, there we were, cooped up in the hot TV room, in the middle of the night, living our best bright-eyed life watching the NBA greats in the nineties. The NBA was only one of the many ways we were, like many young Senegalese kids, living and breathing America vicariously. There were a host of other TV shows that contributed greatly to a very skewed perception of what the United States were all about. We watched the glamorous life of 90210 and Melrose Place after school on weekdays. Dallas and Dynasty had our parents believing Cadillacs only cost $300 in the US.

Then, there was the music: 90s hip hop and RnB with all its swag and style that we worked so hard to emulate. And even if we were huge fans of a deeply prophetic Tupac Shakur, at the time it was the beat and the mostly under-understood rhymes that had us going crazy.

I remember that fateful day in September 1996 when Tupac died. My brother broke the news to me, and we both were standing helpless and devastated in the middle of the hallway at home; I was crying. My mother came home from work to find her two youngest children in a state of deep sadness and was immediately worried.

"What's wrong? What happened?"

"It's Tupac, Ma..." we both whispered.

My mom looked at us both and said, "Tu-who?? Who's that?"

After we explained to our mom that Tupac was this famous American rapper who was shot days ago and just died, she gave us the biggest side eye to topple all side eyes and said incredulously, "Y'all great grandma died and nobody here mopping around. Tu-whatever dies all the way in the US, didn't know either one of you, and you're out here crying and carrying on?? *Yen naka waaney deugg nak!! (You two are truly overdoing things)* ".

Okay, she was right, we were totally doing the most, but in our heart of hearts, we were all a little American inside!

What was so alluring about the United States of America? Somehow, the US had managed to project this image of a country with so much excitement, so much promise, so much good – good food, good movies, good music, good-looking people, good money, and economy. In fact, now that I think back on it, we all would watch gangsta movies like Menace II Society and Boyz n the Hood, where we would see these cute ass bad boys, shootings, and danger, yet it would only make America more attractive, because well... fear is a damn good pull.

The way the USA was portrayed to us on TV seems to have been intentional and misleadingly positive. However, in hindsight, it is clear that the hand of divisiveness was already at play, preparing us to see African Americans differently by overloading us with movies where most of what we saw was them toting guns, shooting up people, being violent, and ultimately forming an opinion in our minds that they were... dangerous and we were different. The real danger is how this brainwashing and molding prepared a new crop of tools; sharp tools of oppression against Blacks in America.

For many of us young Africans coming from the continent, this work that had already been done on our brains. It made us ripe for falling in line in an America that devalues Blacks, discriminates against them, and works hard to destroy their worth and self-esteem. We had been prepared to perpetrate this same hate against our own because we were made to believe we were... different. Unfortunately, too many of us embrace that role too eagerly and start developing a false sense of superiority, then become the worse oppressors to Black Americans, all fueled by white supremacy and its notorious habit to divide and rule. In the end, are we harming ourselves? But we will get back to that!

Then there was the language...while the world calls French the language of romance and deems it one of the most beautiful tongues, French was trivial to us; what we loved was English! Oooh and American English was even better. Spoken fast, through your nose, with curled sounds, colloquial dialect, and contracted words... yasssss!

American English with terms that were not in our British English textbooks but made you sound so much cooler, so much more hip; terms like *what's up* and *yup* instead of stale ol' *howdy* and plain ol' *yes*. Stating that I was dedicated to English is an understatement. I loved the language and I went the extra mile for it: I watched movies and read whole books in English starting in middle school.

By the time I finished Grade 11, I had read the autobiography of Malcolm X in its original published format. I still remember the first word that stumped me: *painstakingly*. I was taking additional American English classes at the time, and my professor, Mr. Ndiaye, taught me to guess the meaning of words using context. Malcolm X was describing his efforts to educate himself while in jail and *painstakingly* was an adjective he used to describe his reading, so appropriate for my case. I kept at it and devoured the book. I developed a deep respect and love for Malcolm X. The little rebel in me was captivated by the story, the cause, the persistence, the virulence, the history... I was, however, far from suspecting that what I was reading remained so painfully relevant and true of the America I was so attracted to. No, never! I read it as a story of the past, a fight that paved the way for this Land of the Free that was my El Dorado. I was in for such a shock. At the time, all I saw was glitz and glamor. That was enough for me to keep pushing this passion until I too could taste the glossy fruit.

My father, on the other hand, was absolutely no fan of the United States of America. Like many African parents, he saw it as a dangerous place where youngsters go to be lawless and lose their virginities and values, if not get killed by stray bullets. He was not having it. America was my forbidden fruit, I felt as tempted as Adam and Eve, and my dad was about to incarnate God and declare *boulko laal boulko djeggee (do not touch it, do not approach it)*.

To understand the dynamics between my father and I, and how it ultimately fueled my attraction and led me down a path following that American lure, you must know who Oumar Gueye is and the history of our complicated relationship.

Oumar Gueye was born at the end of the Second World War in November 1945. It was the end of a world event, but the beginning of the most exciting accomplishment for his mother in her Saint Louis of Senegal household: the arrival of a first-born son, and even though she already had a daughter, this child, this precious son was birthed onto an automatic pedestal upon which he would stay in her heart forever. Oumar was named after an illustrious religious and social figure. One who was as famous as he was respected and mysterious: El Hadj Oumar Tall Foutiyou, the founder of the Toucouleur Empire, which spread across most of modern-day Senegal, Mali, and Guinea. He was a renowned Sufi Islamic scholar, and a recognized political and military leader who was said to perform miracles and whose death was more of a disappearance shrouded in mystery.

Although our own Oumar didn't perform any miracles that we know of, his mother, my grandmother Awa fondly referred to him as "Foutiyou" and venerated him as if he was a reflection of the original. Oumar's father, Amadou, was a stern man, feared even; a hard worker who took his head of household and provider's responsibilities. Emotions and affection were not part of the provision.

As a matter of fact, Oumar spent some of his younger years living at a relative's house where he experienced what we would deem harsh treatment and abuse, but his father would call life lessons and experience. These experiences would insert a seed of nervousness and quick temperedness in the young boy that followed him into adulthood. In his teens and young adulthood, Oumar was a playboy; tall, slim, handsome, and he knew he was too sexy for this life! My dad felt himself so much that he walked with his shoulders at a 30-degree angle, pacing through the streets of Saint Louis, making the young women swoon and the young men jealous. He began a career in the airline industry as his dad was about to retire. This was out of a sense of responsibility after turning down a scholarship to pursue technical studies abroad because he wanted to help carry the family.

My father became a responsible provider at age twenty and that pedestal grew bigger because when you start carrying people, they start telling you only what you want to hear. Oumar increasingly got used to being THE reference, THE voice. He was always right and because his environment also bowed down to him, he got used to getting his way. His opinion and his thoughts were superior and he could not stand resistance or pushback. But the buck stopped at his dad. Despite all his pedestal-living energy, Oumar had a deep respect for his parents, especially his father and did not do anything, not a thing, without consulting him first and getting his blessing.

When he moved from Saint Louis to Dakar and when he wished to purchase a home there, he business-cased his way to his father, who always wanted him to buy or build in Saint Louis and had to convince him of the validity of this home buying plan. Only after his father blessed it did he purchase his first home away from the family's city of origin. By the time I was born, my grandfather had passed away.

My parents had two girls and my dad was about ready for a boy. Uncle Fadel was my mother's gynecologist and a friend of the family. He and my dad found themselves making plans to create a boy: the doctor made my dad quit smoking, put my parents on special boy-making diets, and when my mom got pregnant, somehow, her sonogram revealed it was a boy. Well, it looked like the wanna-be-gods had succeeded in making what they wanted.

My mom bought all blue stuff, hand embroidered baby shirts, and everyone was all happy and waiting for the first-born son. Except real GOD has different plans and had probably been laughing at these boy-making shenanigans taking place before him for months.

On April 28, 1977, at Clinique Yamilé in Dakar at 2:52 a.m., I was born to a resounding "Shit!" dropped from Doctor Fadel's mouth in disbelief. My mom, in a panic asked, "What's wrong with the baby? Is the baby okay?"

Uncle Fadel looked at her and said, "It's a girl…"

My mom replied, "No, it's not…"

Well, yes it was, and it was me in all my glory. My mom got over it quickly and held her baby girl with joy. My dad… well, that was a different story. Uncle Fadel went outside to break the news to him; "Hummm Oumar, huh well, so, the baby is here…."

Oumar was getting anxious because he could sense something was wrong, but he was far from imagining that it had to do with a failure in their boy-making plans. Fadel pursued, "… but it's a girl".

My dad looked at his friend, turned around, got in his car, drove the twenty minutes back to his home, made *ghusl* (a Muslim purification bath) and proceeded to execute two units of prayer and talk to his Lord, whom he interestingly remembered now that his little biology experiment had failed.

He said to God: "Thank you for a healthy baby girl, but God, please bring me a son, and although I wanted a son to name after my father, I promise you I will name that son after your messenger, our beloved prophet Mouhamed Peace Be Upon Him." Only after doing all of this did he proceed back to the clinic to visit his wife and newborn 'failed baby boy', me.

Ooh but little did he know that God works in mysterious ways and that sometimes what you ask for comes, only it does so in a different package than what you expected. What he called a boy, what he willed to become a man, was in fact here; it just came in a format he didn't expect. The glorious package of a strong black woman. Get ready Oumar, the champ has arrived. It's going to be a wild ride!

I did eventually get two younger brothers. The first came three years after me and was named Mouhamed Naby to emphasize that promise my father made to God; *Naby* is Arabic for messenger. Years later, Oumar had a second boy that he proudly gave his father's name – Amadou Abary. He had fulfilled his duty and promise.

As demonstrated by the story of my birth, my relationship with my father started on complicated terms. Interestingly, I was and still am the child who looks the most like him, I am literally the spitting image of Oumar Gueye. I was also the daring child that knocked his pedestal the most or at all.

At age five, when we were living in Paris, after witnessing him slap my older cousin, I flew across the room, grabbed the phone, and started dialing. My dad looked at me incredulously and asked me what I was doing. I recited the hotline number for battered children and said, "I'm about to call them to come get you, you're going to jail! You can't slap Ablaye (my cousin). That's what they said on TV!"

When my dad recounts the story, you can still see his disbelief decades later. He says he felt cold sweat roll down his arms and his back as he talked me out of making the call by using all sorts of bribes and deception. He succeeded but said that day was when he realized this child was going to be his arch-nemesis.

A few years later, when we returned home to Senegal, my dad said that as we touched down at the Dakar airport and exited the plane, he called out my name and said to me, "Welcome to Senegal Anta, there is no hotline for battered children here." Of course, he was being facetious and a little resentful, but I had a complete meltdown and cried my little heart out demanding to go back to France. My father was in fact very rarely physical with us, but the idea of losing my leverage created a power dynamic and recalibration that even at that age I was uncomfortable with. This was probably the beginning of my typical Taurus control freak issues!

Speaking of being physical, the part of my journey to the US that involved my dad did in fact include one of the rare whoopings I remember ever getting from him. Indeed, my fascination with the USA was deep and I had made the unilateral decision that after I graduated from high school, that place would be my one and only destination for college.

I was so sure of this that I started researching colleges as early as 10th grade. I had also convinced my dad, under some false pretense I no longer remember, that I needed to enroll in the US cultural center's American English Language Program. These were the same classes where I learned how to understand words I didn't recognize or know by analyzing their context. The classes were held twice weekly in the evening so I had to catch the last bus home, getting there at night after 8.00 p.m..

When school ended for the summer, my English classes went on for several weeks. My dad who lived in Côte d'Ivoire at the time for work happily paid for these classes, and that summer my mom, who worked for the same company, found herself on a mission to supervise their agency in Guinea-Bissau. She would be there all week, only coming home on the weekends; she left her Uncle Moustapha at home with us to keep watch on the kids. This uncle, the only grandfather I knew, was known for being temperamental and difficult. Even though both my parents knew I was in evening classes, somehow, my grandpa didn't get the memo, and I found out in the worst way .

This was the summer before 12th grade and by early October, the English classes were a thing of the past and we were now getting ready to begin the new school year. My father was home during his least favorite time of year, the days of "Dad, here is (yet) another list of books, school supplies, notebooks to buy". These lists had a way of unnerving him and this particular Saturday, I came into his room with my additional money-asking list and somehow, I put him over the edge.

He threw the money at me, and as I went down to pick it up, he blurted out of the blue with an angry voice: "Don't think I am unaware of how you spent your summer roaming around town at night and coming home at all hours of the evening too!"

I looked up with what must have been an obvious WTF on my face because he slapped me so fast, I forgot what day it was and why I had just picked up money from the floor. I wasn't done with my initial shock when my dad pulled my hair, my brand-new school-is-about-to-start do, ripped four of my braids, and landed a couple more hits while I covered my face from his maniac attack.

I could tell then that he had kept his unspoken anger towards me for months and my innocent little school supplies list was just a trigger for something else. I also realized that my grandpa had been tattle telling to him, probably trying to deserve his little policing job at any cost, not realizing he was reporting a false issue that he could have easily asked me about and cleared up rather than turning it into a discovery or reportable offense.

But I was more upset at my father; he was paying for the classes and forgot that quickly! Was he so eager to find me in something deplorable that he didn't even bother to ask me about these evening arrivals home? Why did he feel the need to keep this so long in him that it rotted into several slaps and an assault on my new-year hair on the most random day?

He wasn't quenched either because after he barked at me to exit his room, I walked back to mine and closed my door. He flew in and marched towards me asking me if I had just slammed the door… which I had not mind you, but I realized he probably wanted to yank the rest of my braids, so I mustered up all the calm in me to answer a whispered *no*. That was enough to send him off. I remember being so angry at how unjust what happened was that I broke a mirror with my bare hands and the glass pieces cut my palms, sending blood running down my skinny wrists.

This was in September 1994. I stopped speaking to my father, other than the necessary hellos, for months after that. I can say the dynamics of our relationship shifted and would always be rocky from then on. However, this was a life changing ass-whooping for me because it somehow opened the possibility of changing my father's mind about me going to the US after high school. After the incident, on top of the silent treatment, I also refused to share meals with him when he would be home in Dakar from his duty station in Cote d'Ivoire, which was generally the last weekend of each month.

As soon as he arrived, I would start eating eggs or sandwiches, or whatever would mean I was not sitting at the communal lunch or dinner. My poor mom would beg me to come eat, and I would say, "I am not hungry".

Although it was clear that was a lie because that was simply impossible for three to four days in a row. I kept that going for his next couple visits and soon my dad started to feel bothered and decided to do what he does best to get his way. In this case, it was breaking down my newly built emotional wall. His tactic was to bribe you emotionally with getting exactly what you wanted in hopes of making you crack. He called home on his birthday, and I picked up the phone; my dad loves his birthday and despises it when people forget. I didn't forget, but everyone else did and maliciously, I didn't remind anyone. I was at war with the man, so any help I could get was fair game at that point.

He went on to ask me, "What date is it today?"

I replied nonchalantly, "It is November 10th, why?

I could sense that dagger going in; my dad asked if that date didn't ring a bell, and I satisfyingly answered "hummm nope". He gave up and asked to speak to my mom. I gave her the phone and walked off without dropping even the littlest hint to her about the missed birthday.

The very next day, I scored my biggest victory yet. My dad called back and gave me a name and a number: Mme Aby Diallo. He said I should call and visit this lady. When I asked who she was, he paused dramatically and then said: "You were talking about going to the US after high school, right? Well, I happened to meet this lady here in Abidjan, and apparently that is what she does for a living as an academic advisor. You can go see her so she can orient you in your process."

I was flabbergasted, but cautious. I knew my dad and was aware he was trying to get me to soften up with my Cold War. At that point, I knew he had just opened a door I needed to rush through fast and conquer before he decided to shut it for whatever reason.

I called and visited Mme Diallo within a couple of days. And this woman, the outcome of my life-changing-beating of September 1994, ultimately became the wind beneath my wings and sent me flying towards Lady Liberty. Mme Diallo became my advisor and through thick and thin, worked her hardest until my dream came true fourteen months later. This didn't come without its share of drama, and I will get to that.

The year before this, the theft of my heart was already complete. After successfully finishing 10th grade with a principal's prize, a vacation to my coveted destination accompanied by my two besties was a gift from our parents. I visited Washington DC and New York City the summer of 1993 and the lure became a full-blown pull as we became mesmerized by skyscrapers, huge stores, fun activities, and what to us at the time was amazing food. All the while, forgetting that vacation and living were often different, and we were in fact seeing the shiny side of the coin.

SAD 2: The Pull

Shooting down red flags for the sake of love

A lot had happened in the 10th grade year of 1993 leading to my first visit to the United States of America. Before ever reading the autobiography of Malcolm X and believing things had changed since those days, my friends and I formed a gang of almost twenty and went to the movies in Dakar to watch the notorious Denzel Washington play brother Malik El-Shabazz in the epic Spike Lee movie.

We rebelliously, loudly boo-ed and kept disrupting the room, as uncomfortable white moviegoers started exiting the theater during the film. Eventually, an attendant had to come and ask us to calm our zealous energies or leave.

Once we got called to order by the theater attendant, our rebellion turned into wide-eyed young girls' admiration, a safer emotion if we were going to finish watching this movie without getting kicked out of the place; and we swooned at the handsome Denzel Washington and echoed *Amen* in chorus as he recited an impeccable surah al-Fatiha, the beautiful opening chapter of the Holy Quran.

We had always been an excited bunch and since we were also Catholic school girls whose head nun was known as one of the most severe principals in town, I suppose our degree of *rakaju* (overexcitement) outside the confines of school tended to be exaggerated since we were always operating in a heavily regulated environment.

Short of a school uniform, we wore a long, blue, sleeveless buttoned-up shirt over our clothes and got in trouble if the buttons were left open. I will always remember one of our most notorious surveillants, Mme Diompy, posted up at the entrance of the middle and high-school section of the school, scrutinizing every one of us as we entered the establishment, and ensuring our 'blouses' were buttoned up all the way.

13

She also ensured our skirts were long enough and that we were always dressed appropriately. Mme Diompy would not hesitate to send you home to change or on dismissal for a mini skirt or a midriff shirt, the infamous 'Madonna-top' as we called it growing up in the *Like a Virgin*, 80s era.

All these rules and stringent regulations undeniably gave us much pent-up anger that we could not express at school. Although many of us tried, and it made us quite the rowdy bunch when we were out of the claws of our surveillants and away from the walls of our establishment.

We walked away from watching the Malcolm X movie full of pride for his fight towards justice, and sorrow for his cowardly murder. Although we felt a sense of solidarity and understanding, we were still so naïve. And so far from imagining that the 50s and 60s world we saw play out on the big screen was trying to raise red flags for us revealing that the condition of Black people in America was not pristine and that the US was not an equitable place for all.

I didn't see or didn't want to see those flags. I loved my America, and she could do no wrong in those days. I was in the pull and anything that was trying to negate my ideal was to be categorically ignored.

This was also the year we learned, and had to recite in English class, Rev. Martin Luther King's *I Have a Dream.* In hindsight, we learned that text completely out of context – which is one of the unfortunate issues with our francophone education system of the time.

The emphasis was more often on learning things by heart in order to regurgitate them versus developing the proper understanding and relevant analysis that knowledge required to become truly potent. In rare instances, we would have teachers who were truly pedagogic and took time to explain, contextualize, and plant a seed of passion about their field in our young brains.

English teachers were a hit or miss, but I had my own seed of passion growing in me for that language. So, even when I had an English teacher I despised, I still excelled because it was already my favorite subject.

When I was in school, English started as a mandatory subject in middle school, whereas nowadays kids in Senegal are taught English very early, some as soon as pre-school. Our first English teacher lasted less than a week. Even though we could be a tough crowd, I have to say her premature departure was not our fault. She was a young white lady with a Senegalese married name, and she didn't speak a lick of French. This could have been a benefit in the higher grades where kids had some bases in the language but for our first experience, this was torture. The first day of class, she went around asking our names in English. We all had an idea of the correct answer to give, either from TV or by figuring it out after the first few answers that the teacher was saying "what's your name?"

It was a hilarious exercise because some of us, instead of giving our names in its correct pronunciation, were trying to show off our potential knowledge of English alphabet, often gathered by personal interest before entering middle school or by listening to songs, and would mispronounce our own name adding As, Is, and curling sounds where none existed.

Beyond the introduction segment of our new class and teacher, the remainder of the hour was a mess. We couldn't understand the teacher, she couldn't understand us. The first time we were exposed to English instruction was supposed to be exciting. Soon enough however, it became an agitated and frustrating sign language class where neither students nor teacher made any progress.

After a few days, there were lots of complaints and probably several angry parents calling the school to demand their hard-earned coins spent on one of the highest tuitions in town be honored with a proper English teacher for their children.

We were introduced to a new teacher: my future enemy, Mme K. She was a beautiful, vibrant Tunisian woman and she spoke French and English perfectly. Her teaching style, however, was not as beautiful as her appearance. She would scream at us at the top of her lungs and repeatedly call us imbeciles for any small mistake we made.

I quickly and increasingly grew frustrated with this lady despite being one of her top students. I loved the class but really despised the teacher and my budding social justice self could no longer stand to have insults and screams hurled at us daily when we were doing our best to master a language that wasn't our own. I decided to report her to the lead teacher, our French instructor, who by the way didn't treat us much better. At least she limited her terror to demeaning comparative comments between students of different levels and shouting at us constantly. She became our English teacher in the following grade on top of French and here we were exposed to double abuse. My courageous "I'm gonna utilize 'the System' in place to get us justice" did NOT work as expected.

Apparently, 'the System' did not have a built-in confidentiality clause or whistleblower protection measure and somehow Mme K knew exactly what happened and who reported her. This was the beginning of a long love-hate relationship between us. I was excellent at English and being a good student gave me the latitude to act a total asshole right back to her. She targeted me and I reacted right back, acting like the mafia gangster I wasn't but enjoyed making her suspect I might be. I would arrive in class, put my books on the table, cross my arms, and stare dead in her eyes all class long without flinching once.

I am not even sure what I was trying to do but to me this was having a destabilizing effect and sending her a message that I was not afraid of her or affected by her insults... except I probably was and my way of coping was to rebel against the woman teaching what happened to be my favorite subject.

No doubt she would have loved to fail my defiant little self, but that was my upper hand; I loved English and I was good at it, never hesitating to give it extra efforts in and out of school. I had Mme K twice in middle school and once in high school as an English teacher. Our relationship never really normalized, nor did her abrasive attitude.

With time and growing up, we came to realize that her angst and constant lashing out wasn't necessarily directed at us but was rather a reaction to deeper, darker issues she seemed to be having at home. Something we saw play out through the bruises on her face more than once. It was in her high school English class that we learned the famous *I Have a Dream* speech.

I Have a Dream was taught to us as a text of victory and pride as opposed to the cry of despair and strong denunciation pronounced by Martin Luther King on those iconic steps in Washington, DC. We had to memorize a good chunk of it and come to class ready to emphatically recite it in front of everyone, placing emphasis on words we had not yet fully grasped and wrapping it up in the emulated ardor we heard in Reverend King's voice.

We were so far from really understanding the magnitude of the words we were speaking.

Back then, we couldn't comprehend how relevant those words were as we were dropping them, thousands of miles away, standing before our teacher and classmates in Senegal. When learning the speech, I particularly loved that part about being judged not by the color of one's skin, but by the content of their character.

In my case, the color of my skin was the majority in my country, so my main reason for pounding the words so hard when reciting them was a slight to Mme K, a white skinned Tunisian that had us sometimes wondering whether she was mistreating us because she might be racist.

I also connected with King's depiction of a world where children of all color, faith, and backgrounds would unite and be free. After all, I was one of the students that organized a rendition of Michael Jackson's *Heal the World* at our school's annual dinner-spectacle as an ode to peace and unity.

I was an early activist, which my parents repeatedly confirmed by telling me stories of me as a very young child seeking justice and equality for various people in different situations that often were none of my actual business as a kid. *I Have a Dream* should have been yet another red flag about my beloved America; but we were judging her against Beverly Hills, Melrose Place, Dallas, and Dynasty, and other shows where Cadillacs cost 300 dollars and America was the El Dorado.

And we chose THAT dream, eclipsing King's, and erroneously presuming his as mostly attained. I feel like at the time, what was most important for us, and maybe for our teacher too, was being able to recite a text in English, kill it in phonetics, pronounce words correctly, and be flawless at grammar.

No one was expecting us to deeply analyze racial themes and discrimination when regurgitating a powerful text. English was after all our second language and we were not expected to do what we did in French class, where we deeply analyzed and wrote elaborate texts and opinions – yet, that technically is also a foreign language to us even though we were born into it, but that's another story for another day!

Unfortunately, the red flags and my insistence on ignoring them, and sometimes even mocking them did not stop at the depiction of real life on the big screen, or speeches from activists relating challenges in America. My classmates and I were also exposed to first-hand accounts of these challenges, and we shooed those away too.

Mr. Diop was our history and geography professor in 10th or 11th grade. He was a big guy, very tall with dark brown skin. We liked him a lot because not only was he fun, made us love his subject, but he also spoke fluent English and when we were learning lessons with English words, he pronounced them with that 'from the nose curled sound' of an American accent that impressed us every single time.

This was not by chance or because he may have been a good student in school; in fact, Mr. Diop spent some time in the US as a student and oooh did he have incredible stories to tell! I will never forget the one story he told us that we mocked and dragged him for filth for. In hindsight, twenty years later, it made so much sense... too much sense.

We were studying the USA and its states; in fact, we had to memorize all of them, their capitals, and know how to place them on a blank map, the same thing we had to do in geography for each continent, including the Americas.

As we were discussing the states, Mr. Diop would give anecdotes, pointing out what each was known for and their notable monuments. When we got to Detroit, MI, our professor's anecdote was downright dark and scary. He described it as the most frightening experience of his life. He vowed to never forget it. Right there, before he even started, we decided he was about to amplify something and tell tales because never had we seen big, tall Mr. Diop say anything about being scared, and we didn't think he could be.

He went on to explain how one day he was walking in town minding his own business when several police cars with alarms glaring surrounded him, cops pulling up with their weapons drawn, and he was told to get on the ground. Needless to say, we were all glancing at each other like, 'what movies does Mr. Diop think he is playing in right now?', we were incredulous. He explained that he automatically complied but was completely lost because he had no idea why the police would stop him, let alone in such a grandiose way when he hadn't done anything.

He said they approached him and asked for his identification, which he told them to get from his back pocket since he was lying face down with his hands on his head. When they did, he said they realized they mistook him for someone else who looked like him and let him go.

Oh, the class went wild! We were cackling and short of calling him a liar. We let Mr. Diop know we did not believe a word he said.

We told him his story sounded like some Hollywood gangster movie and we just could not for the life of us fathom that this story could happen to someone in real life, especially someone WE knew. Nah, as far as we were concerned Mr. Diop was out here telling tall tales and trying to impress us further than words so we could worship his aura more.

I decided to shoot down this red flag too and dismiss it as an attempt to tarnish my dear USA. Not having the slightest idea that years later, while living in my El Dorado, I would see Mr. Diop's story unfold over and over and over again, only those times, the many Mr. Diops did not survive.

I didn't have to wait too long for the first instance of these horrendous stories, as NYPD officers Sean Carroll, Richard Murphy, Edward McMellon,

19

and Kenneth Boss killed an unarmed Guinean immigrant, Amadou Diallo, with 41 gunshots on Feb 4, 1999. A mere two years after I arrived in the US as a student.

But back in middle and high school, you could wave a sea of red flags in my face, and I would choose to ignore them and stay loyal and dedicated to my love, my America. I must say she was doing such a great job luring and pulling me with our local media mostly helping her by perpetuating her filtered messages to us, glamorizing the USA as the land where *everyone makes it*.

For me, at the time, the USA also represented a nemesis to France. I was a Senegalese girl living in a former French colony, with a rebellious streak and an avid attraction to Pan-Africanist and revolutionary leaders of the continent like Thomas Sankara and our very own Cheikh Anta Diop, one of the biggest Egyptology experts I have ever known. Colonization was a common trauma for many Africans and though much more pronounced today, with a better understanding many of us have of geopolitics and the way power systems and dynamics work on the global stage, many of us carried a certain rancor toward the former colonizing metropole.

In my case, I also carried a bitter first impression related to France that has never left me: I experienced my first racist event there at age five on my first day of kindergarten in Paris. I went from a vibrant pre-school in Dakar where most kids looked like me to a huge school in a cold place where I was only one of four black children from Senegal; my older sister and I and another set of girls who were also siblings.

Our family moved to France for reasons I would only discover many years later; at the time I was an excited five-year-old moving to a new country with my parents, my two older sisters, and my baby brother. We were accompanied by our aunty, my dad's cousin who had been living with us for a while and one of his nephews he decided to take along for better educational opportunities.

The real reason for the move was more devastating; my mother had breast cancer and my father decided to take a pay cut at his job and move us all to

France to a lower position available for him in the company so she could be closer to her treatment center. And so we went, and arrived in France for a new adventure, just a few days late for the start of school.

My oldest sister and my cousin were middle schoolers, and their new academic abode was on the other side of this huge school. My second older sister and I, who were three years apart, attended on the same side as the other set of Senegalese siblings in kindergarten and elementary.

As we arrived that morning, clutching each other's hand, my sister and I were welcomed by a school staff member, said goodbye to our aunty and mom, and headed separately with a different adult to our new environments. Kindergarten for me and second grade for my sister.

I vividly remember entering a class with that adult who turned me over to the teacher with an introduction that butchered my name. That teacher presented me to the class of wide-eyed white children as the newcomer "from Africa" – as if I didn't have a specific country of origin – and pointed me to my seat, a few rows back from the front.

As I walked to that seat, I passed a little blond girl with a round bob and big blue eyes who looked at me and said loud enough for me to hear, "Espèce de noiraude" which practically translates to "damn nigger". Yes, a five-year-old white child called another child 'nigger" *in kindergarten*... I was bright enough to know that I had just been insulted, but I simply looked at her long enough to remember who she was, and proceeded to my seat without a word, and that was done... or so blond-bob-blue-eyes thought.

At recess, when all the kids were in the recreation area playing, I spotted blond-bob-blue-eyes; I started running towards her. My sister saw me and started instinctively running towards and then behind me. The other set of Senegalese siblings, for whatever reason, followed suit. I jumped on blond-bob-blue-eyes and started fighting her with all my five-year-old little rage and big might. My sister and 'adopted sisters' stopped, watched, and without even knowing why I was fighting this girl, egged me on instead of pulling me back.

We went on full survival mode, and it was "one of us is mad, we are all mad". The brawl didn't last long and soon school staff came, pulled us apart, and here I was in the headmistress' office on my first day of school… so much for a discreet entrance: late and making trouble on day one.

My mom was called, and I am so glad she knew her children well and wasn't one to get intimidated. As soon as she arrived, I first got 'the look' (so I knew right then I was in big trouble once we got home). But when the headmistress explained that her daughter jumped a kid for "no reason", my mother looked her straight in the eyes and said: "Had you said that her older sister fought, I would be tempted to believe your account, but this one is not one to fight at all, so *for no reason* makes no sense in this case. Have you asked her WHY she fought this kid?"

My mom was right, I was all mouth, but I was not a physical fighter at all! Even so young, I was the biggest strategist but none of my scheming included physical fights, at home or elsewhere. I remember my dad telling that infamous story of his dinner guests gathered in our living room early into our arrival in Paris, and me sitting in a corner with an open book 'reading' out loud from it and turning pages accordingly. They exclaimed and oooh'ed and aaah'ed about his preschooler reading perfectly.

He laughed and told them I wasn't reading yet, to which they responded that I was obviously reading the words and even turning the pages appropriately. He then explained that what I did was observe when an adult was reading that book to me, and memorize the story and the breaks, and came there sitting and emulating it all as if I were actually reading, when in fact I was scheming. And I can assure you that DNA is a strong defining link because my daughter did the same thing at age five, decades later!

My mom knew my strategic streak, and she was well aware that it must have taken something big and overwhelming to get to me and make me act so out of character. When she discovered that the adults at the school had not done any sort of investigative confrontation between my 'victim' and I, she demanded that they ask each of us what happened to determine the facts before proceeding to next steps. I explained that my classmate had called me *"espèce de noiraude"* and the girl actually confirmed it, showing she probably didn't comprehend the magnitude of her words and was probably just repeating how she heard other people – whether her parents or else – refer to people who looked like me.

The headmistress was as red as a pepper and my mom was fuming, I could tell, even though she kept her legendary regal posture. She would recount to us how she told the school staff present that she would not tolerate her children being treated as automatic aggressors nor would she want them in a school that didn't have better ways of dealing with racism. They offered endless excuses and apologies. Blond-bob-blue-eyes became one of my best friends for the remaining years we spent at that school in Paris.

However, that experience never left me and taught me that racism was learned and often passed down, dangerously able to create people who carry it naturally without identifying it as such until shit hits the fan. Some will recognize and work hard at unlearning and then fighting it, and others will scream foul telling you their best friend or even spouse is black or brown and rebel against it.

At any rate, this early experience of France turned me off and made it easy for me to develop a rancor that led me to skip the French universities' opportunity fair in high school where many of my friends received the valuable information on which schools were available for us as non-French citizens and even which universities would welcome us at low to no cost. I spent the fair outside at a snack stand enjoying a chocolate brioche and a Coca Cola and dreaming about universities in my destination of choice and destiny.

The decision had been made; higher education would happen nowhere else, and my Holy Grail became an acceptance letter to an undergraduate university in The United States of America.

So, after all our drama, when my dad introduced me to Mme Diallo, I took full advantage of it and rushed to see her so she could make my dream come true.

SAD 3: The Fight for America

You shall not stand between me and my love

Mme Diallo's office was in her home compound and happened to be walking distance from our house. On the day I went to meet her, I had my precious folder filled with months of research on various universities and programs. I had my excitement and hopes, but most importantly I had the drive to succeed that connected our two souls at the very first glance. Meeting 'tata Aby' as I affectionately came to call her was an act of God and felt as such. I arrived at her home and was led to a waiting room where I sat, anxiously waiting to meet my *Messiah*.

In hindsight, I have to recognize that one thing I always carried was a certain level of Black pride. This pride had been gathered from several areas:

- My admiration of Black leaders like Malcolm X, Thomas Sankara, Patrice Lumumba
- My love for Bob Marley whose lyrics of Black power uniting I sang with heart and belief all through school
- My values and history learned from the elders in my family who spoke of our ancestors and their might and fearless battles

My mother's family descended from the valiant Malian Emperor Soundiata Keita through their matriarch Koura Souko, who married their patriarch Pourdasse Diagne, a Black Algerian soldier and they started their family in Saint Louis, Senegal. My father's family came from a long line of warriors and royals from the Kingdom of Walo in the north of Senegal.

That sense of self and belonging compounded with the influence of diaspora Black pride gave me a strong foundation. However, it still didn't make me see myself as merely 'Black' – a skin color, but rather 'proudly African'. The multiple red flags that life was throwing up for me against my beloved America went unnoticed and ignored.

That pride, present in me, even influenced my early research on universities in the US. In fact, I had started researching Historically Black Colleges and Universities before heading to my first appointment with Mme Diallo.

Morgan State University was high on my list of choices tucked in my nice stack of neatly cursive-written notes. I had spent long hours researching and jotting down these notes, sitting in the American Cultural Center's library with that huge encyclopedia-sized book of colleges and universities.

As I sat in Mme Diallo's waiting area, I saw many young students like me. All clutching their documents, eyes full of hope, waiting as I was to meet the key to that coveted door to their American Dream.

Students were going in and out of her office, many accompanied by parents whose faces often were not as elated as their kids'. Probably because as the students thought about The American Dream, the parents were thinking about how much that would cost them and the hole it was about to burn in their pockets. We were here to go at it the legal way, seeking to further our education in the USA and that did not come cheap… not at all.

My father was quite aware of this well-known fact and how it might factor into his finances and budgeting. But as I mentioned before, introducing me to Mme Diallo was more part of a ploy to return me to his realm of influence than it was a genuine act of support for my own ambitions.

This would become clear very soon for me as I engaged in this intense yet exciting process. I was so early it was ridiculous, but also the parents and students spent significant time inside speaking to Mme Diallo. And so, after some time in the waiting room, it was my turn to enter the office. My heart was beating so hard I thought it would pop out of my small teenage chest; this was like meeting a celebrity you had long been a fan of and finally getting a chance to speak to one on one.

Mme Diallo was a sweet woman, about my mom's age, with such a calm and reassuring aura that I immediately felt comfortable and soothed. My heartbeat slowed back to normal and somehow, right there even before we said anything beyond hellos, I felt like my dream had just found its open door.

We sat and spoke for a while. Mme Diallo asked me questions about my plans and objectives, where I saw myself in a professional future, my current standing in school, and whether my parents were supportive even though she understood my dad connected us. It must have seemed odd that I showed up alone at this very first meeting when other students attended with one or both parents.

Quickly, I explained that my mom was at work and dad was abroad but assured her that my father was aware and supportive of the process and pushed me to schedule the meeting to speak to her about my desire to study in the US.

I then showed her my research and the list of schools I had already targeted as being of interest to me. She zoomed in on Morgan State and asked me why I had selected it. I immediately answered, in my most confident voice, that it was a Black school, and I would probably feel at home there. Somewhere in me, I suspect that I was still traumatized by that Paris experience of racism in a foreign country. Maybe I was trying to recreate my own environment elsewhere to prevent a repeat.

Clearly, having much more experience than me, Mme Diallo explained something about not pigeonholing myself based on a school being 'Black' and suggested I select a non-specific school. Evidently, I had no knowledge of the strong legacy surrounding Historically Black Colleges and Universities, and I probably didn't even understand exactly what it was Mme Diallo was trying to either explain or protect me from. But at that point, this was Master Dream Maker and whatever she said was 'gold' to me. I returned home with a shorter list of universities and a task to reflect on and decide from it.

I loved the Georgetown University Hoyas so that made it my top pick! My second pick was attended by several kids who had sat right there like me in Mme Diallo's office, Townson University. Both were in or near Washington DC, where I had vacationed and fallen deeper in love with the US a couple years prior.

The final selection, a couple of weeks later, included a funny episode where I learned you cannot teach an old monkey new tricks. I went to my dad when he returned on his next trip home and revealed the final two to him with my need to make a choice. Obviously, from a parent's perspective, there was no financial comparison here with Georgetown easily being twice or thrice as much as Townson yearly. For me, I was also looking at the coveted top tier school on a resume and which doors it could open later when it came time to look for a job.

My dad then asked me, "When you finish your Bachelor degree, what do you intend on doing?"

I thought about it for a second, knowing my dad was always all about school, school, school and his girls being financially independent before thinking about marriage. I replied, "Of course I will keep going and do a master and then a PhD!" ... I fell right into the trap he set!

He laughed and exclaimed, "There you have your answer! Who the hell is gonna look back at where you got your bachelor's degree when you have a PhD? You should keep the top tier school for your terminal degree, it'll make way more sense that way."

I knew I had lost that one and simply acquiesced and made the choice: Towson University it was. Mme Diallo took the time to provide me with all the required costs for my list, and my dad asked me how much it would cost him; I answered that (at the time) it would be around 10,000 USD a year. He crossed his leg on top of the other, looked at me smirking and said: "I will pay, not a problem; but on one condition: I expect you to pass your baccalaureate exams *with honors*."

I still don't know whether this condition was because he honestly didn't think I could do it, given that honors were quite exceptional at that level, and he thus believed that would get him off the hook. What I do feel is that he obviously didn't know me well enough to realize that I hated being challenged and all it took was to tell me *you cannot* for me to fight tooth and nail to disprove it.

At any rate, despite the sunken heart in my stomach, I assured him that he could start putting the money aside because I was going to bring that baccalaureate with honors he just requested, God willing. As I walked away, a small nagging voice inside me screamed, "Girl, you know good and well that your pitiful math grades will make the honors level unattainable for you."

The voice was not lying, I was horrible at mathematics and that was a known fact to all! But thank God for the roaring fire inside me that sent up flames of abnegation and covered that voice of doubt with: "This is what you want, and it will not come easy, but as long as you believe and work at it, it is yours to lose… do it!" I chose to garner fuel from that inner fire and promised myself that I would work like I never had and make the dream happen. Interestingly, it was a very good friend of my dad, tonton Demba, who helped me; he found me painstakingly studying one Saturday at home and happened to be the math genius I needed. He made it his business to turn my fate around and came every week to tutor me. Math problems used to look like Pharaoh-time hieroglyphs to me, yet he taught in a way that seemed much more understandable. I started solving them with ease to my own great surprise.

The combination of my determination and my very visible efforts in what was my subject of doom must have caused an alert for my dad because on one of his trips, he enigmatically came and found me reading in my room and said that I needed to go see Mme Diallo as soon as possible. I was confused because we didn't have a meeting scheduled and there were no immediate tasks I needed to go there for. He insisted and added that she needed to tell me something. I was intrigued and headed over to her place that same afternoon.

Mme Diallo welcomed me with her usual motherly care, but I could see in her eyes that something was wrong; she looked worried and sad at the same time. As we sat in her office, she started by telling me how impressed she was with my drive and all the efforts I was making and that she knew I was someone who, if given the fraction of a chance, would be focused and successful if I went anywhere… and then she broke the news.

My father had been there to speak to her and said he could no longer commit to the financial responsibilities of me going to Townson University. He explained that being the father of five children, he had thought about it and couldn't reconcile investing so much money on one of them to the detriment of the others and felt that it was just too expensive and somehow unfair to my siblings.

I was at the crossroad of crushed, angered, bewildered, and disoriented. I didn't understand the logic in my dad's argument considering he was well aware of his circumstances when he told me in a solemn, crossed-legged posture that he was going to pay no problem. I was angry that he didn't tell me himself and sent me to my Messiah to receive such betraying news.

I was sitting there shaking because I didn't know what this meant for me and my dreams. It was literally a couple of months before my baccalaureate exams. My eyes welled up as I tried not to let tears flow, but the pain was stronger than me; I felt like a thief had robbed me of my most precious jewel, I started crying. Mme Diallo quickly handed me tissue and said, "Don't despair Anta, I have already thought of a couple of solutions! You have made a mark on me and no matter what, I will support this dream of yours until you get to the US. Please go home, speak to your mom, and tell her to come here with you as soon as she can find the time."

Moms have been the s-hero without a cape for many families in Senegal. Many spent their last dime doing what today would be seen as asset planning. Buying gold jewelry and keeping it stashed for rainy days, working hard at many informal activities alongside their formal jobs to make ends meet or save money, participating in money saving and lending groups, etc. My mother was no exception.

After our dad moved to Abidjan for his job, she was raising all of us, assuming daily runs to and from school, working full-time as a mid-level executive, and concurrently making good use of her time off to travel and purchase clothes and shoes that she sold to her circle of friends.

My mom was a wonder woman. She was not a hugely communicative mom when we were younger but with time became a confidante because she was always supportive of our efforts and goals and praying fervently for our success. We saw that daily. I remember vividly, on schooldays, the routine of waking up at dawn and stopping in her room to greet her on our way to taking a bath.

Every morning, we would find her sitting on her prayer mat, basmala beads in hand, worshiping and making dua (prayers). It seems my mother never missed her morning appointment with The Creator and that image stays with me to this day, decades later, as I pray in the morning and my own daughter comes in to say her morning hellos.

Truly an anchor in our extended family, my mom organized family events and together with my dad they hosted a New Year's Eve Ball at our house every year for as long as I could remember. She was the treasurer of her multiple savings and lending groups because of her ironclad reputation of honesty and organization; she was a confidante for many of her friends and blood or soul sisters; she was generous, beautiful, and kind.

My mom was a community momma, and we wouldn't fathom the true magnitude of that truth until she passed in 2018. Her funeral gathered an unimaginable number of people, many of whom we didn't even know, who related all kinds of stories about her discreet humanitarian and philanthropic actions.

Mme Diallo, a mother herself, knew all too well the power that make-it-happen moms yielded. She knew that summoning it to my rescue would bear fruit and lead to the positive outcome we sought. When I returned home from my fateful impromptu meeting, I went quietly to my room, grabbed my book, and continued reading with a sore heart and red eyes.

My dad came by and stood at the door to ask whether I saw Mme Diallo. I nodded. He asked if she had told me. I was tempted to say, 'Told me WHAT? Why couldn't YOU tell me this yourself when you're the one who put this whole process in motion? What kind of coward move is this?'

But I refrained, both because I knew saying that out loud would probably land me at the cemetery and because I didn't want to claim defeat. So, I quietly answered that Mme Diallo had indeed told me, without either of us ever actually saying what the *thing* was that I had been told.

My dad said "…and?"

That felt like pouring salt on a fresh wound, like what do you mean *and? And* I'm mad, *and* I hate this, *and* you betrayed me, *and* I haven't even brought up the condition you asked for yet, *and* why are you doing this, *and* what type of manipulative bullshit is it, *and???*

Instead, I said, "… and I heard her and understand your point, thanks anyway. I, however, will keep researching for other ways because this is my future, and I must be proactive in making it happen." That's what came out of my mouth and that was it. He tried to explain something but honestly my eyes were down into my Agatha Christie book, I was nodding at random and had already stopped listening to him.

To me, I had just been betrayed and fooled. I was determined to get what I wanted without him at this point. It had become a challenge bigger than the baccalaureate with honors. The fire in my belly was now roaring through my whole body with a hunger to prove to my dad that he didn't rule the world.

He had already played God by trying to create a baby boy back in the late seventies and failed. I was about to serve him another failure in the mid-nineties by being who he thought he could prevent me from becoming: an international student all up in Uncle Sam's land.

My mom knew my dream and it didn't take long at all to convince her to come with me for a meeting with Mme Diallo. It only took a few days before I was back in the room with my now co-conspirator. This time with my mom in tow for an epic, female pow-wow. The sole objective; setting me on a path to success.

Rarely have I felt this much genuine support as I did in knowing these two women, each powerful in their own humble ways, were combining their might – ability, love, and prayer – to surround me with positive will and incredible efforts because they believed I could do it.

I am convinced that this particular time in my life has contributed precious fuel to my inner fire every single time I felt like giving up or was discouraged. This level of trust and support was enough to last you decades and deserved nothing else but your chin up and eyes forward, always.

Unknowingly, this act of love amplified the grit that has always been mine and strengthened me as a young woman.

Mme Diallo quickly explained to my mom the situation and the turn of events with my dad suddenly backing out of his previous commitment. She laid out the costs and options, and also mentioned a delegation which was coming to Dakar in a few months from a different university in Florida that she wanted me to meet. Mme Diallo was in full-on networking mode and somewhat saw in me a level of hunger and persuasion that encouraged her to fight for a young woman she had met only a few months prior.

My mom listened thoughtfully, and I could almost hear the calculator in her head adding up savings, side business profits, potential loans, and new revenue-generating ideas... She was insanely concentrated on Mme Diallo's words, but I knew deep inside, the same fire that burned in me once again lit up in her, and she was wracking her brain on how to ensure my flame didn't go out.

Once tata Aby finished exposing the issues and options, my mom stayed silent for a while. Finally, she looked at me, then at Mme Diallo and said, in the voice of a determined queen prepping her troops for war, "Inshaa'Allah (God Willing) and may He give us life to see it, Anta you WILL pursue your higher education in the US even if it takes my last dime. Mme Diallo, what are our next steps? Let's get this child on her way!"

THAT was my mom! I was elated and at the same time humbled and choked up. I knew she didn't have half the means my dad did, but I had also seen her silently getting people out of financial trouble, using her money for good, and being a beacon of hope for so many.

I knew that God blessed her, and she would find our way out of this trouble because what goes around comes around, and my mom made good go around. My mother, a woman of faith, strongly believed in the power of prayer and she made it her most efficient weapon. I know she pulled that weapon out and sharpened it for this fight.

Sometimes, I could see her looking at me while holding her basmala beads with this willpower in her eyes, and just knew my mother was formulating the strongest and most sincere prayers for me to succeed, for us to succeed. And boy, did we!

The baccalaureate exams were just a few weeks away and I think this meeting countered the disappointment of my father's announcement leading to the challenging couple of weeks of examinations. I remember coming home from the mathematics afternoon test; my hair was disheveled, and I honestly looked spent.

My mom was on her prayer mat, awaiting my arrival with visible anxiety she didn't show for any of the other tests that week. When she saw me, she couldn't help but stand up and ask, "… so?"

I smiled, despite my obvious mental exhaustion, and said, "Ma, it was hard, but it was just like what I worked on with tonton Demba in the past few weeks, and I really think I did well!"

Mom high-fived me out of excitement and sent the maid to buy me a cold coke! She was that excited and I will never forget that feeling of seeing her so proud of me, which with mom wasn't rare; she may not have been super communicative on life stuff when we were younger, but she always expressed her contentment and pride for us.

My inabilities in math were a bit notorious at school. In fact, when I finished 9th grade and succeeded in those state exams, I had a dilemma and my mom, once again, had come to the rescue.

I was attending one of the best Catholic schools in Dakar with my sister and our high-school didn't have a literary and language department, like the A-series or L1 available at other schools in the area. Languages, however, were my biggest strength. I did not want to pursue that field though, I wanted to go to the Economics department called B-series or ES, in which I was heavily influenced by my dad who was a Finance Executive.

34

At the end of middle school, students received orientation towards the department that seemed to best fit their profile and grades, and I received an A-series orientation. This meant double disaster for me: I was not going to pursue what I wanted to do, and I would have to change school away from the only friends I knew considering this was the only school I had attended since our return to Senegal from Paris.

I was livid and I quickly started telling my mom that there was no way under God's sun I would be going to any other school but this one or doing anything other than ES. My mom was a ride-or-die, if you liked it and backed it up, she loved it and fought to make it happen. But you had better NOT embarrass her after she had engaged in that fight and she made that clear to me: "Anta, I hear you, but you know Mother Superior (our headmistress and a very respected and borderline-feared, Mother Superior nun at school and around town) is not to be messed with. If I go there defending you, you'd better be sure I will not tolerate you failing if she accepts to keep you in ES!"

Swearing on my kidneys and unknown future first-born child, I guaranteed my commitment to this cause. So, there we went to a meeting with the daunting, and legendary Mother Superior. She sat stoically behind her wooden desk, with her impeccably white nun garments, a few strands of red hair poking through the front of her veil, and her piercing eyes looking straight at me.

I was intimidated but not scared to defend my cause. After the usual greetings, my mom explained the reason for our visit and the fact that we wanted to revisit my orientation to L1 by exploring a change to ES, which matched my ambitions better.

Mother Superior thanked my mother, turned right to me and said, "*Mademoiselle* Anta, you know better than me that ES requires a certain level of mathematical ability that you do not have. How do you think you might make it in ES with these... pitiful grades of yours in math? Why would you not take advantage of the fact that you have excellent language abilities and shift your ambition to more guaranteed success?"

Yes, Mother Superior never minced her words and she had just obliterated me by calling my math grades pitiful, but she was telling the whole truth! I garnered all I had left in dignity and courage, and without hesitation, I explained to her that I had the passion and drive necessary to turn my math grades around.

All I wanted was a chance to prove that I could succeed in 10th grade ES. Mother Superior looked at me for a long time, sternly but with a spark in her eyes. She then turned to my mom and said soberly that she would give me that chance, however, if my grades were not up to par, she would kick me out of school quicker than I could say the word *math*.

I didn't know if I was more excited or scared. Either way, I was relieved that I could stay for high school with the only academic institution I knew besides my far-away preschool in Dakar and be with my friends. I also realized the gravity of my situation and made it a point, in good Taurus fashion when challenged, to prove to Mother Superior that I could. Once again, I was hugely grateful to my mom. She stood up for my conviction but also reminded me throughout the school year ahead that I had a challenge to prove myself and she believed in me.

I ended 10th grade in the top three of my large 30+ student class and received a prize from the hands of Mother Superior herself. What a way to rise to the challenge! Even though Mother Superior wasn't one to show much emotion, I could see in the faint smile she gave me when handing me my stack of prize books, that she was proud of one of her girls. Her school promoted excellence, and I had just proven that I did indeed belong there.

A couple of years later, this determination may have been part of my validating proof as a fighter, because once again, my mom was by my side as we left Mme Diallo's office to fulfill my destiny. I went on to pass my baccalaureate exams with honors, which I took extra delight in announcing to my dad as he sat eating lunch with his friends and almost caused him to choke on his rice.

But because my efforts to join a university were thwarted at a critical time, I now had several months to kill while working on a new process of applying. I took that time to improve my English with classes at the

American Cultural Center, and studied for my TOEFL and SAT, all with the unrelenting support of my mom and tata Aby Diallo.

Our trio's marching orders did not include the possibility of NOT succeeding.

Mme Diallo was working on receiving a delegation coming from the University of North Florida for a visit to Dakar. Meanwhile, my mom and I were running around town getting my vaccines up to date and prepping documents needed as I started working on an application to Townson. That application, however, never made it to Maryland. In fact, Mme Diallo had spoken about me to people from the Florida delegation and created an opportunity for me to speak to one of the school's representatives and executive, Dr. Betty Flinchum.

The conversation, anchored in my desire to learn economics and development strategies from what was known as the first economic power of the world and bringing those skills back to benefit Africa, must have impressed her.

Soon after they returned to Jacksonville, I received a call from Mme Diallo. She asked me to come back with Mom for some good news. I was excited but cautious because I had no idea what such news could be, considering I had not yet sent my Towson application and I knew talking to someone couldn't mean I was on the plane to Lady Liberty. Mom and I sat before Mme Diallo with trepidation and waited to hear the news in question.

I could sense the happiness in her voice when she started speaking, but also a sense of pride as she looked at me and said, "Anta, your belief in yourself paid off and I am so proud of you. Dr. Flinchum was so impressed with you that she invited you to apply for the Florida-West Africa Linkage Institute scholarship at the University of North Florida in Jacksonville. They think you fit the profile of the students they are seeking to welcome and I couldn't be happier for you."

I thought I was going to die of joy at that moment, and I started crying and laughing at the same time. My mom's first words were *Alhamdulillah* (Thank God) and she then expressed her gratitude to Mme Diallo for materializing the wonderful opportunity.

She turned to me and said, "Anta, God has cracked the door open for you, and now you must work hard and walk through that door with the same grit you have displayed to date in order to benefit from that divine gift."

I passed the TOEFL and SAT with flying colors and worked on my application to UNF. I remember the topic of my motivation letter being to speak about a famous person that I found inspiring. My choice was Mahatma Ghandi and the steady picture that had been drawn for us in school about his relentless yet peaceful approach to liberty which earned him a Nobel Peace Prize.

I wrote a poignant, but in hindsight naive, essay about him and how his satyagraha philosophy was one that I believed could heal our world and strengthen the bonds of our humanity. Little did I know that my hero had a sinister past as a racist.

His troubling early stance on race, as described by his biographer Ramachandra Guha, was that Africans were uncivilized and surpassed by Indians, and that Europeans were the most civilized of all. He used choice words in his early 1900s writings describing Black people as "… troublesome, very dirty and liv[ing] like animals."

Ghandi was also seemingly pro-apartheid affirming that white people in South Africa, where he wrote from in 1903, should be "the predominating race". According to his biographer, Ghandi did go on to drastically change his views and spent the better part of his famous life as an advocate against discrimination of all types and as an anti-racist. This gives us hope that there is movement possible along the spectrum. However, the responsibility to educate oneself about anti-racism must genuinely come from within and not be thrown on external sources to bear, including those who are victims of racism and discrimination, as is often and unfortunately the case nowadays.

If you are on a genuine journey, you must hold yourself accountable.

I had more hurdles ahead and one more disappointment awaiting on this long strenuous journey to my beloved USA. My dad had been observing me and my mom running around like chickens with our heads cut-off and he just knew we were up to something. He was also incredibly annoyed that he was not totally aware of the details of our many trips to Mme Diallo's office and our million errands that included me coming home with a freshly vaccinated arm.

One day, he called me out to the veranda, and said, "I see you and your mom coming and going and I just know you must still be working on this *going to the US thing.* I am the head of this household and I need to know what exactly it is you're up to, what's going on?"

This was after I had sent out my UNF application but before I heard back about the scholarship. So, I told him that, like I had said when he backed out of his commitment, I had continued looking at options and that Mme Diallo had found a few that Mom and I were exploring together. I, of course, couldn't help being petty and added that I didn't think I needed to tell him any more about that since he made it clear he wasn't paying university fees that high for one of his children when he had several.

My dad then asked me the weirdest question ever. I wasn't sure if this was another trap or if he was being serious; he inquired: "So if these options pan out and you get a concrete opportunity to go to the US, would you still go if I say *no?*"

I looked at him incredulously, not understanding why he would ever ask something like that, and responded with all the calm I could muster. "Well, as you said you ARE the head of this household, so I suppose if you tell anyone not to do anything, we would comply. However, I can't see you telling me not to go, especially after seeing all my efforts and the time spent making my own objectives happen. I wouldn't know how to even qualify that, Dad."

He thought for a quick second and laughed, saying he was just kidding. When the announcement of my approved application and scholarship came, my dad suddenly became all excited about the results and said he was willing to pay for the fees alongside my mom.

In the end, our combined efforts, and my application to the University of North Florida (UNF) succeeded. I was accepted on a scholarship that allowed me, an international student, to pay in-state tuition for four years, thus exponentially reducing the financial burden of this dream of mine. Although this was a huge relief, it was still going to be a stretch for my mom. She committed to making it happen and off we went with the planning for the Fall 1996 semester.

They worked out some sort of combined payment where my mom still had to fork up a few thousand dollars a year; I promised her that I would work and continue seeking opportunities when I settled in to make things easier. I thanked them both for their support, even though my mom got the largest part of my gratitude for sticking by me through the rough roads to glory.

All that was left was the I-20, the precious document the university sent alongside the official acceptance letter which allowed each international student to get an appointment at their local US embassy for the infamous F-1 Visa Application, the final step to the coveted departure. The process for the Visa application was stressful. There were many steps, checks, payments, and an interview where you were left to defend your dreams and convince the embassy that you were not trying to move to the US and never come back to your own country.

That perceived goal seemed to be standard for every single interview and you were sure to get bombarded with questions on why you were going, why you selected your university and major, what your plans were afterward. The interview was filled with all sorts of traps to check your willingness to return to your country of origin.

In my case, however, my I-20 was sent by UNF but for some reason didn't reach me for weeks. I was beyond stressed. The school sent me all the information on how it was mailed and who the carrier was so I spent every day for weeks sitting on a chair outside our house's main door, watching the street and looking for anyone or anything that looked like a postal carrier. The fall semester had already started and there I was, outside our house in Dakar, waiting for my I-20.

The more days went by, the more it seemed obvious that my fall semester entry goal was faltering; arriving for a semester that had already started as a brand-new international student didn't scream set up for success. My mom and Mme Diallo conferred with the school, and we decided together to defer my admission to the spring. It wasn't ideal but it was a simple delay in my journey. I strongly believed, like my mom, that everything happens for a reason.

My I-20 ultimately came, and in the funniest of ways. I was at my regular surveillance post outside the house; at this point, I was so regular in my duties that people who didn't live in my neighborhood were probably impressed that there was a female guard outside the house. So, there I was sitting and watching the road, when I saw a gentleman walking with a large red and yellow envelope in hand labeled AIRBORNE and my brain automatically sounded an alarm, because that was the carrier's name the university gave me.

I jumped up and ran after him, yelling to catch his attention. As I approached him, he asked me, *"Khana yow yay Anta Gueye?"* (Could it be that you are Anta Gueye?); I jumped up and down and said, "That's my envelope! That's my I-20! Where have you been?"

The gentleman looked amused and explained that they had been looking for my address for weeks and that they somehow couldn't find it because our strip of houses didn't show up in their system as part of the official postal address lot, which threw them off.

I wasn't listening to half of his words; I was too busy hugging the large envelope to my chest and thanking God for bringing it before my next deadline. My battle crew got our ducks in a row, yet again and my mom and I headed to the US embassy for my visa appointment. I remember my interviewer being so young I wondered if he was an intern there. He was pleasant and spoke directly in English. I responded to his questions

41

thoughtfully, and he noted that my English was as neat as my document folder.

Then came the trap question: "What are your intentions after you earn your degree and why did you choose Florida?"

I looked him dead in the eyes, and said: "Did you see the temperatures outside of Florida at this time of year?" He laughed and that relaxed the exchange a bit. I went on to explain that I chose to major in Economics because I wanted to learn from the best in order to be in an advantageous position to help my own country to further develop. He noted my scholarship and congratulated me on that, and I said with a smile, "Now you know the number one reason my *parents* chose Florida!"

The other interviewers I could hear speaking were not as nice or relaxed, and some were even quite arrogant and mean. I felt bad for the gentleman next to me who was a green card holder and was accompanying his brother to get a tourist visa; he was denied right there on the spot and the interviewer said to him that he didn't believe his brother intended on returning. The kid was in high school. I was luckier as my interviewer told me to come back that afternoon to pick up my passport and visa.

I walked out of the room and smiled at my mom with tears in my eyes. She smiled back, tapped me on the back as I gave her a thumbs up, and said "Thank God, I guess this is His time, the right time!"

SAD 4: Coming to America
When the eaglet first landed

My mom and I landed in New York City a few days before Christmas 1996. Saying my goodbyes in Senegal was such a happy moment for me. I gave my teddy bear collection to my sister and cousins. My mom's friends brought me all kinds of gifts, including trendy winter clothes and a big, beautiful coat I would never need in Florida.

The weather in New York that winter was icy, however, and that coat came in very handy as we did our last-minute shopping for our trip to Jacksonville. I had never been to Florida and neither had my mother. One of my uncles had said, on his visit before my departure, that Jacksonville was the largest city in the United States of America. I was intrigued and inquired whether it was bigger than DC and New York, to which he answered affirmatively.

The then nineteen-year-old girl in me was super excited because I started imagining a giant Times Square where I could continue having my vibrant social butterfly life alongside being a student. Little did I know 'the largest city' was measured by land mass and not bustling entertainment and in the case of my new home away from home, the disillusion would be quick.

We departed NYC LaGuardia to Jacksonville, FL on December 30th. As the flight approached its descent, I looked around outside my window and all I saw were trees everywhere; I couldn't see a *city* anywhere.

I turned to my mom and asked her where the city was. Ever the optimist, she said to me with so much conviction that I couldn't help but believe her: "Remember what your uncle said about Jacksonville being the largest city in the US? I am sure this allows them to place their airport far from the center of the city and the habitations to avoid crash zones, that's great!"

My mom worked at the now-defunct biggest multinational airline on the African continent at the time and was always very sensitive to issues around airports being too close to where people lived, given that takeoffs and landings were the most dangerous times of a flight.

Our home in Dakar was not very far from the airport back then, and when my mom had to pick up someone coming in by air, she would sit in the yard and wait to see their flight landing before heading to the airport. She would always mumble about how convenient yet dangerous our area is. She called it a 'crash zone', in response to our giggling jokes about her fear of planes despite years in the industry.

I analyzed my mom's answer about this large city affording to put their airport out in the middle of nowhere as a safety measure. I agreed it made sense and breathed a sigh of relief that would be short-lived.

We landed in Jacksonville dressed in our cold NYC gear, and they opened the plane door. The first two things I noticed were how hot it was for a late December morning and the strong smell of sulfur. I decided right then that this city was not going to be my friend. My mom and I headed into the terminal, and I found a phone booth for us to book a hotel.

Not knowing the city at all, and remembering my school catalog, I presumed the school was near the ocean and decided the hotels in the area called Jacksonville Beach would do. We picked one, arranged transportation, and headed over.

Now, anybody who knows and remembers Jacksonville, FL in the late nineties knows that the beaches were one of the rare walkable places in the whole city. So, my mom and I were not getting a real feel for Jacksonville as we decided to spend the next couple of days in that area before move-in day and the international students' orientation on January 2nd and 3rd at the University of North Florida.

While at the beaches, we walked to get food and look around and one day even walked for hours all the way to the highway junction on a hunch from my poor map-reading skills. I thought we may be able to walk to the university and check it out before Dr. Flinchum picked us up on move-in day to drive us there. Needless to say, that was an epic fail as I severely underestimated how big this place was and the map's scale feature.

We spent New Year's Eve eating pizza in our hotel room and watching the ball drop in Times Square on TV. On New Year's Day we made phone calls back home to wish everyone good tidings for 1997. The coveted day of my move-in arrived and Dr. Flinchum picked us up from the beaches and got on the way to UNF.

As she drove, I kept looking at this long stretch of asphalt, Beach Boulevard, on which I noticed nothing exciting besides a Regal Movie Theatre on the right side and trees and bushes. At the time, Jacksonville was wide and empty, and I was not impressed. We took the turn on to Kernan Boulevard to get to the back entrance of the school. There was a big apartment complex on that road called Melrose Place that made me smile. Trees, trees, and more trees. I was getting more and more nervous, but I could see my mom smiling and seeming quite appreciative of what we were seeing. We got to the school, and I was confused and excited at the same time.

We had just driven at least thirty minutes and the school I saw before me looked like it was nested in the heart of a thick forest... *Why did the school magazine that came with my acceptance letter have students with surfboards and show buildings that looked to be by the seaside?* Yes, you guessed it, I had just been introduced to good marketing and Photoshop!

Nevertheless, I was happy that I had finally arrived in my new home away from home and I couldn't wait for what was next. My mom was leaving that night back to New York, so she went through orientation with me and met my three roommates who were from Thailand, Guatemala, and Ethiopia.

One of my roommates later told me that she had been debating with her sibling whether my mom and I were another sister pair and was shocked to learn that the other 'young woman' was my mom. Of course, Mom loved that anecdote! After the orientation, we moved into the Osprey Village in a duplex with a two-bed room on each floor, a kitchen, a living space, and a bathroom.

As freshmen, we would have been obligated to spend at least one academic year in the dorms before getting a chance to apply to the village. However, international students were allowed to live in the apartments in their first semester to have access to a kitchen to make their home foods and alleviate the challenges of adapting to a new culture.

Once my mom and I had a chance to tour the university, meet with key folks, and she saw me settled in, she was satisfied and ready to go. But she didn't do so without finally giving me the explanation for all those smiles and appreciative nods she had been serving that morning.

My mom looked at me and said with a straight face, "this place and this city are exactly what your social butterfly self needs to keep a focus on school. If I hear that you even attempted to transfer *anywhere* other than this place before you finish your 4-year degree, you are coming right back to Senegal on the first flight out of here!"

I could tell she was serious, and right then and there I started hating Jacksonville, FL with a passion for coming between me and my social opportunities. Little did I know I would make so many amazing memories and friends in this city, see it grow in superb ways both in infrastructure and culture and that it would give me the best college experience ever. But before it got good, I had to go through some rough patches of culture shock.

My Test of English as a Foreign Language scores landed me the opportunity to start college courses right away without going through a semester of English as a Second Language class. This was a relief in many ways since it would reduce the cost for my parents and prevent any wasted time earning my degree. But it did make me work twice as much in the first months because those professors sounded like they were speed-talking to me! I purchased a mini tape recorder and for at least a month or so, I would record my professors in each class, and replay them at home to cross-check my notes.

Eventually, I got used to the Southern drawl and speed of speech, but it took me a bit longer to understand Black slang, *Ebonics*. When you mixed the two, Southern accent and Ebonics, I was sometimes left wide-eyed, nodding, and shaking my head at the same time. Wondering why, with a near-perfect understanding in English, I could not make out half of what I was hearing.

The culture shock of the different expectations and ways of studying came at me fast and furious. Used to writing cursive, I remember turning in my first English Literature paper beautifully handwritten to a teacher who incredulously looked at me saying, "What is this?" and explained that all papers had to be typed.

I would from then on handwrite my papers first, then take them to the typewriter room, and painstakingly type them with slow, two finger taps to meet the professor's expectations.

With time, I migrated to the computer lab and eventually reached the point where I started thinking in English and writing my papers directly from the keyboard onto the screen. My familiarization with both *Ebonics* and African American culture came from my on-campus job as an assistant at the Student Development Center. I sat at the front desk on the ground floor of the building, and assisted students with submitting flyers for distribution, renting out rooms for events, getting information on various clubs and activities, etc.

In the position, I interacted a lot with students from various backgrounds, and also with club leaders, including fraternity and sorority students. I was popular with the guys with my tall, slinky, chocolate self, and my shift made the front desk a buzzing meeting place. The constant interaction was beneficial for my colloquial English and soon, I too was saying things like *whassup* and ending my sentences with ... *and shit*!

The most unpleasant part of the onboarding into my new life was the constant need to answer questions I really didn't expect from college-level students. I remember when we first traveled to DC on vacation, and my friend's brother explained how his college mates were asking him how he got to the United States, and his favorite answer was to say he swam through sharks and crossed the Atlantic.

Little did we know then that he was *not* joking about those types of questions, but also that his answer was actually true for some people who chose to migrate using rudimentary boats, and often ended up fighting for their lives in the middle of the ocean trying to illegally reach what their El Dorado and hope for a better life was. My fellow international students and I did not escape the questions.

And after trying to give sensible answers at first, out of annoyance, my strategy too was to be petty.

I was asked how I reached the US and replied that I swam. I was asked whether I started wearing Western clothes because I came here to attend school, and I would say that I actually did bring my dried leaf skirts and coconut bras for the weekends.

People wanted to know whether it was true that we lived under trees in Africa, and I replied that it was, and my dad's tree was right next to the US Ambassador's tree in our village. I could not believe the basic and ignorant questions I was hearing from students who were attending university. Many of them honestly believed that Africa was a neighborhood and that all of us, no matter what country we were from, knew each other somehow.

I was at my wits end when my roommate from Ethiopia and me, from Senegal – literally two totally opposite countries geographically on the continent – were asked if we knew each other *back in Africa.* At first, we laughed but when we realized the white girl asking was dead serious, I unleashed the pettiness and asked with as much solemnity: "Do you know Jenny?" She looked at me and asked who that was. I said, "Jenny from California! You don't know her?" The girl smiled and said she didn't know anyone in California.

Irritated, I explained to her that Senegal and Ethiopia were much further apart than Florida and California, so how then did she expect my roommate and I to have known each other? But that was without realizing that my interlocutor had zero idea of geography anywhere outside of her own city, let alone a whole other continent.

This became painfully evident as I watched one of my favorite TV programs back then. It was a game show that had a trivia component which happened outside with random people and the contestants had to guess which passerby would get the answer right.

In one of the episodes, the street mic guy asked several people to name three *countries* starting with the letter 'I'. Shockingly, many of them actually gave *states* as the answer, and did so confidently: Iowa, Idaho, Illinois…

Watching US television gave me a better understanding of why so many people seemed to know so little or have such skewed views about the world outside the USA. At the time, I saw a lot of Discovery Channel and National Geographic shows that presented a very primitive side of Africa, Latin America, and Asia. They would feature tribes and places I had never encountered in my entire life.

I would later get into a tense exchange in graduate school with a visiting guest in our course on Management of Nonprofit Organizations at The George Washington University. The guest was a marketing executive at The National Geographic in Washington DC. After she made her presentation to the class, we had a short networking session where I approached her for a chat. I introduced myself, told her I was from Senegal, and quickly explained to her my experience with the absurd questions I was getting when I first came to the US as a student.

I told her that I started by being mad that people would ask such things, but that once I started watching her channel, I understood that people were simply reacting to what was being fed to them on TV and asked if she felt National Geographic had any responsibility in this miseducation. I also asked her why, given they were investing so much to travel to these remote areas to feature primitive ways of life, did they not provide the other side of the coin by also featuring the modern life they crossed all throughout Africa, Latin America, and Asia to reach their final destinations.

I was known for asking tough questions and not being afraid to call people out to debate around difficult issues, especially when it came to development and cultural competency. My professor saw this from across the room and hurried towards us, probably suspecting I might be giving our guest a hard time.

The executive smiled and asked me whether I wanted the commercial answer or the real one and that she assumed I would pick the latter, which I did. She then said, "Viewers don't want to see what they already know, so showing them the modernity of African cities doesn't sell; they want exoticism and things that are at a polar opposite of their lives, that's why".

I thanked her for her candor and added: "You presented your channel as educational, yet you just said that providing balanced information so as not to misrepresent the continent I come from doesn't sell. In that case, what makes you different from MTV or VH1, because it sounds to me like you're more into entertainment than education?" That was the moment my professor pulled me to the side for a fake chat that was in fact intended to get me away from the guest.

At UNF however, my international economics lecturer would often turn to me and say "Anta, take it away…" when someone in class would start a debate rooted in paternalistic or imperialistic absurdity. Such was the case when two students who had been in the Marines started saying that life in America wasn't comparable to the 'uncivilized' places they had seen around the world.

The professor then asked them to define *uncivilized* and one of them said that these places and cultures were barbaric. "Anta take it away…" led to a debate between me, a few other international students and the two former Marines. I pointed out that their definition and judgment upon other cultures were exactly the same energy and sentiments that started imperialism, slavery, and colonization. That attitude and ignorance feeds racism; culture could not be judged as barbaric or uncivilized unless the one doing the judging is positioning his/her culture as the superior and correct standard by which others should live.

Growing up in Senegal most of my childhood meant seeing people like me as the majority, and also as standard role models. They were the leaders of our country, they were the CEOs of enterprises, they were presidents and ministers, etc. They were leading political and social movements. But it also meant being taught history that valued who I am, my ancestors and their fights against colonization, leading figures of Africa's rich past, and warriors, kings, and queens who in their own ways revolutionized societies and marked our lives.

My education included learning about more modern leaders and activists who always refused the notion of Africa and Africans being somehow lesser than a Caucasian culture or civilization that had positioned itself as the standard in a world where its people were in fact *the* minority.

I grew up looking up to leaders like Cheikh Anta Diop who debunked all the planted stories white washing Egyptian history and proved that it was in fact Nubian. I was taken by the activism and Pan-Africanism of Thomas Sankara and Patrice Lumumba, but also the temerity of the women of my ancestral Walo, in the North of Senegal. They refused to be put in servitude by colonizing forces and burned themselves because they valued their human dignity first and chose death over rape and subjugation.

At ceremonies, griots would sing the praises of each family's history and ancestors and tell their exploits; you couldn't help but be proud! Sometimes it would not even be a griot, but one of the family members who was known for their exceptional knowledge of the family tree.

In my mother's family, that was my Aunt Nafy, and it was always a proud joy to hear her speak of our ancestors and the lineage my family had to the valiant and mystical emperor Soundiata Keita of Mali whose descendent Koura Souko was the matriarch of the family

This foundational self-esteem built into every little Senegalese child was important for me. I would only realize it once I moved to the United States of America.

I was a very active college student. Mme Diallo had trained me well, teaching me that college was not just going to classes but also getting involved in student activities so that I could build up a strong resume and also learn the complementary skills that one needed in addition to academic competence to succeed in life.

So, I was everywhere. I applied and was accepted into the Presidential Envoys, becoming an ambassador of the school, and getting amazing hosting opportunities with dignitaries like the Board of Regent and t also university visitors like famous author Elie Wiesel. I was on the leadership team of the International Student Association, a member of the African Student Association, and president of the Economics Club. I participated in the Volunteers Student Association, and was very involved in all school activities, ranging from Homecoming to debates of ideas.

I never shied away from approaching my professors for advice on ways to get involved and sharpen my skills. Any clubs I could engage in or publications I should read, I followed up on their recommendations. Office hours helped me to get a deeper understanding of topics of interest and opportunities to interact with them as experts. I was genuinely curious and an avid learner, and that energy opened many doors because who doesn't appreciate a student who loves to learn?

In these many roles, I interacted often with other club leaders, and that is how we started discovering the unspoken tension between African and African American students. We all got along well, but when confronted by deeper debates, we would find that there were many obstacles to the two groups really becoming one.

The respective presidents of the African Student Association and the African American Student Union decided to call a summit with the club members that would allow us to hash out our perceived differences. The summit was called Closing the Gap and would be an eye-opener for me and a small window into how much the US was doing to make sure Black people would not unite in the belonging idea of being ONE people.

Our club volunteered to cook for the event and we made a spread of delicious and various foods that anchored the discussion as we all munched and debated on very sensitive issues, all in a sociable fashion that made tense moments easier to bear.

And some of the moments were in fact quite tense, like the one where our counterparts had two members bring up that one of the issues one group had against the other was that our *African ancestors sold them into slavery.* An argument I heard many times after, and sometimes even coming from Africans themselves as a guilt-ridden observation placing the blame of Africa's dispersed children on its own and sole shoulders to bear. Except that argument has been strategically manipulated to give it amplified focus while deflecting from the actual horror of a *race-driven* Trans-Atlantic slave trade.

Denying that forms of slavery existed in Africa before the Trans-Atlantic slave trade is impossible; in fact, slavery existed in some form in most areas of the medieval world, including in the former Roman Empire whose decline marked a receding practice of Europeans owning other Europeans as chattel property, starting in the early 400 A.D. into the 1200 A.D.

As their contextual socio-economic and political environment progressed, Europeans started focusing more on owning land and the output of its production rather than the labor that produced it; slavery then was converted into systems of serfdom that granted laborers rights that slaves never had.

Similarly, in Africa, slavery in pre-triangular trade often resulted in groups becoming captive to the winning side of political or economic conflicts who then used them as prisoners of war for labor, to expand their nation, to spread religious beliefs, and sometimes as trade currency for economic purposes. Unlike in the European system, the elite groups in Africa placed less importance in the ownership of land, which was open to agriculture and not necessarily divided into individually owned parcels; rather, their power was in the control of labor which led to the ownership of production.

However, an enslaved individual in this system lived with a certain degree of flexibility, was integrated into a community, was not necessarily separated from his kinship or familiar environments and land, and mostly, was more likely to gain freedom within their lifetime. The concept of race did not generally determine rights, although the remnants of this system still pollute modern society in the different forms of caste hierarchy found in several African communities today.

When plantation agriculture rose in the 16th through 19th centuries as the key tenet to the world economies around the Atlantic, the transatlantic slave trade created more demand for slaves. A more extreme form of slavery rose within which humans became movable commodities across distant locations, and their race became a token of inferiority that decreased their status and stripped them of any rights.

A vicious circle formed with European slave traders, knowing they could not amass the quantities of captives they needed for this new intensive plantation economy without the help of African middlemen. They created the demand for and supplied the goods from Europe that the middlemen and their chiefs would purchase with slaves using their known routes but this time trading men, women, and children to white men on the coasts.

But trading trinkets was only a small facet of this new system; the exchange was not always willful and raids to capture slaves became routine in areas on and around departing coasts of Africa. Once these captives changed hands, their whole status would take on a new meaning and their race became a factor that equated them to lesser than human, simple commodities, rightless creatures that would be put to work without compensation and into cruel servitude that violently dehumanized them with no hope for freedom.

This shift was created, maintained, and nurtured by the Transatlantic slave trade and that racial burden hardly lies on Africa's shoulders to bear. In fact, there is enough evidence in the written records of ship captains to demonstrate that even in the reported human trades on the coasts of Africa, there was not a general acceptance for slavery on the part of Africans and lots of the transactions were built on the Europeans' perfidy, deception, and greed.

A famous example is that of King Nzinga Mbemba of the Kongo and his relentless series of twenty-four letters to Portuguese King João III which he began writing in 1526 to decry the apparent subterfuge the Portuguese undertook to fuel the slave trade from his Kingdom. He condemned the importing and spreading of controlled substances into his land, creating addictions that led thieves and bandits to raid and kidnap kingdom inhabitants and trade them to the Portuguese merchants in exchange for the goods they desired.

King Mbemba also recounted broken promises from the Portuguese monarch that youngsters turned over to their merchants would be trained and returned to the Kingdom. King Nzinga Mbemba, who by then had been convinced by the Portuguese missionaries to adopt Christianism and the name Alfonso I, wrote the following:

> *"Sir, Your Highness should know how our Kingdom is being lost in so many ways that it is convenient to provide for the necessary remedy, since this is caused by the excessive freedom given by your agents and officials to the men and merchants who are allowed to come to this kingdom to set up shops with goods and many things which have been prohibited by us, and which they spread through our Kingdoms and Domains in such an abundance that many of our vassals, whom we had in obedience, do not comply because they have the things in greater abundance than we ourselves; and it was with these things that we had them content and subjected under our vassalage and jurisdiction, so it is doing a great harm not only to the service of God, but the security and peace of our Kingdoms and State as well.*

> *And we cannot reckon how great the damage is, since the mentioned merchants are taking every day our natives, sons of the land and the sons of our noblemen and vassals and our relatives, because the thieves and men of bad conscience grab them wishing to have the things and wares of this Kingdom which they are ambitious of, they grab them and get them to be sold; and so great, Sir, is the corruption and licentiousness that our country is being completely depopulated, and Your Highness should not agree with this nor accept it as in your service. And to avoid it we need from those*

Kingdoms no more than some priests and a few people to reach in schools, and no other goods except wine and flour for the holy sacrament.

That is why we beg of Your Highness to help and assist us in this matter, commanding your factors that they should nor send here either merchants or wares, because it is our will that in these Kingdoms there should not be any trade of slaves nor outlet for them. Concerning what is referred to above, again we beg of Your Highness to agree with it, since otherwise we cannot remedy such an obvious damage, Pray Our Lord in His mercy to have Your Highness under His guard and let you do forever the things of His service, I kiss your hands many times.

Many of our people, keenly desirous as they are of the wares and things of your Kingdoms, which are brought here by your people, and in order to satisfy their voracious appetite, seize many of our people, freed and exempt men, and very often it happens that they kidnap even noblemen and the sons of noblemen, and our relatives, and take them to be sold to the white men who are in our Kingdoms; and for this purpose they have concealed them; and others are brought during the night so that they might not be recognized.

And as soon as they are taken by the white men they are immediately ironed and branded with fire, and when they are carried to be embarked, if they are caught by our guards' men the whites allege that they have bought them but they cannot say from whom, so that it is our duty to do justice and to restore to the freemen their freedmen, but it cannot be done if your subjects feel offended, as they claim to be."

["Excerpt of letter from Nzinga Mbemba to Portuguese King João III", in World History Commons, https:// worldhistorycommons.org/excerpt-letter-nzinga-mbemba-portuguese-king-joao-iii [accessed January 24, 2023]

During our Closing the Gap Summit, when the issue of Africans selling their peers into slavery came up, the tension was so thick you could cut with a knife. My African students group stumbled trying to respond to the statement, and some simply agreed. Others who were probably a bit more read on the topic, attempted to explain the chattel slavery system and conceal the more horrific side. Africans weren't responsible for that. Europeans created and nurtured slavery for centuries on all of our backs.

I don't remember there being any resolve on the issue but talking it out in the open was somewhat cathartic. It allowed the two groups to bring up a key problem that was often thought of but unspoken, and it created a dialogue that was healthier than keeping resentful feelings toward each other. This debate also prompted me to want to know more about African American history. I began to ask more questions, read more, and explore what it had been like for Black people in America. I started to step outside what was mirrored to us abroad, to understand their lived experience from an authentic perspective.

In hindsight, I guess it didn't take too long for small unseen and unfelt cracks to appear in my beautiful American Dream ... cracks that my future experiences, different events, and a consistent curiosity would deepen progressively, over many years.

Until the dream would eventually shatter in my hands, heart, and soul.

SAD 5: From Petty to Wise

Discovering the seeds of white supremacy

Moving from Senegal to Florida for college was a culture shock to say the least.

However, it was also a great learning journey. The direct interactions with Black American students taught me a huge amount about a culture that might not have been mine but had similarities that made it relatable.

Following the Closing the Gap Summit between the African Student Association and the African American Student Union, my on-campus job at Student Affairs gave me more opportunities to interact and grow my network. I was aware of all the clubs promoting diversity, the Greek societies, events, and gatherings to attend, and of course who the leaders were of these student associations and their cabinets. This is where I started meeting more people and engaging in mutually enriching conversations, including many about how life was for me back home versus in the US, debunking many myths along the way.

It wasn't lost on me that the image of the US in Africa was centering on Black America either in an overly glamorized and exceptionally attained Hollywoodian life through sports and music or in a violent life through movies. Meanwhile, in the US the ploy was to center African lives as the source and cause of slavery. This was ultimately pitting both groups in an adversarial stance that would create tension and difficulty when they met.

It looks like the white supremacy seeds of division had been planted and at play for longer than I suspected.

By mirroring the Black American experience as *undesirable* to Blacks outside America, the root of an evil plan to use non-American Blacks as a tool of oppression against Black-Americans was set in motion. How many African parents, seeing the skewed violence in films, would have made up their minds that their child should not hang around Blacks in America for fear they would get shot, be exposed to drugs, be courted by gangs, end up dropping out of school and going to jail?

How many parents, even now, try to distinguish their African kids from Blacks in America by telling them they're different, when in fact in the eyes of 'the System' (or the police), they aren't at all? How many Africans in America to this day look down on the Black American community, and on the other hand, how many Black Americans still get offended and vehemently push back when they are told they originated from the continent?

Those coming to the US would be used to oppress those living here, and the latter would be rightfully offended that the immigrating Blacks were benefiting from the long and hard, abolitionist and civil rights struggle of their ancestors throughout the years without giving due respect. Quite a number was done psychologically to separate and divide us, to ensure we were set up to fight each other as enemies or adversaries.

As long as we let our history be told by others, the version that will be presented and held as truth will always benefit them. When history is written by those that oppress, raid, and colonize our lands:

The actual truth will remain veiled.

It is critical that African history be told from the vantage point of African historians and researchers and integrate it into curriculums. This ensures that our children and descendants learn our history minus the control and manipulation of colonialist systems.

When it comes to slavery, there were countless movements of resistance on the continent with leaders and warriors fighting ferociously to protect their people and communities from the Triangular Trade horrors. Some like King Alphonso I of the Congo, started participating but later reneged and fought to protect his people as he discovered the ruse of the Portuguese to keep their trade going. Others were fierce opponents to the European slave trade early on.

In Senegal, history tells us of the reputed first democratically elected Almamy, (King of the Fouta Toro region) Abdel Kader Kane. Coincidentally, Senegal is where the famous departure slaves' fort and home of *the door of no return* sits, off the coast of Dakar on Gorée Island. [source: https:// jikapost.com/histoire/abdoul-kader-kane-le-premier-almamy-du-fouta-toro-par-papa-gora-diop/1107/]

Almamy Kane first rebelled against the Trarza Moors to end the practice of slavery and their extortion of his lands' resources starting in 1786, before turning his fight towards neighboring kingdoms of Kajoor and Waalo which were steady in supplying the Europeans with slaves. Almamy Abdel Kader Kane was known for his disagreements with the coastal town of Saint Louis where countless European traders were residing.

The Almamy fiercely opposed the transatlantic trade, and his laws required commerce ships crossing his territories through the river Senegal be systematically searched to enforce his prohibitions of human cargo going through his kingdom. The Senegalese Almamy wasn't alone. Other documented opponents of the Atlantic slave trade include King Ansah of the Gold Coast (modern Ghana), Queen Njinga of the kingdom of Mbundu (modern Angola), and King Agadja of Dahomey and Agor Akoli of the Ewe people, (both in modern Benin).

It is unfortunate that the imperialist-led narratives are so engrained in history that even on the continent, during tours of the Gorée island slave fort, young local guides rehash the version blaming Africans for slavery to tourists coming from all over the world and barely talk about African resistance (although well documented) or the many leaders who opposed the transatlantic slave trade.

Bob Marley's *Redemption Song* inspires the idea that we must emancipate ourselves from mental slavery. It is high time we take the reins in recounting our history and owning its narrative because, in the wise words of John Henrik Clarke:

"To control a people, you must first control what they think about themselves and how they regard their history and culture. And when your conqueror makes you ashamed of your culture and your history, he needs no prison walls and no chains to hold you."

There is another layer to the whole dynamic between Africans and Black Americans, and that is the discerning types and levels of trauma each group carries that plays into their life experience. In fact, I often say that Africans have a shared trauma inflicted by imperialism and colonization. Meanwhile, Black Americans combine the shared trauma of an ever-morphing Jim Crow AND personal trauma of just living while Black in America, having to constantly navigate the threats of police brutality, institutionalized racism, and discrimination. All of these adversaries can affect them individually and totally derail or sometimes even prematurely end their lives.

When we arrive in the US as Africans, we come with the foundation of having been told all our lives who we were, where we came from, the warriors and great kings and queens who preceded us and their accomplishments. We come with this strong self-esteem instilled in our very bones and we are determined to face the new environment with laser focus on success and only success.

We do not (yet) have the pressure or specter of individual racial trauma and for many of us, we are able to navigate through college before ever discovering it. Some continue to live sheltered enough to stay oblivious to the challenges faced by Black and Brown folks in the US, but even then, too many racially charged events happen daily that must scream to them that something is definitely not adding up between these incidents and the beautiful "land of the free" vibes we were consuming before falling into Lady Liberty's arms.

And speaking of the infamous *system*, I used to hear my college Black American friends mention this often as being the root cause of all evil and the reason behind disparities affecting their communities. At the time, I didn't grasp it entirely. It was either 'the System' and/or 'the Man'... I kept pushing and asking what those were and how they could be so powerful as to undermine a whole segment of society. I naively wondered how come I wasn't being stopped by them too.

But surely, as time went on and my life in the US took form, I would soon meet both 'the Man' and its 'System' and understand the side of my beloved America that she so craftily kept hidden from me during our courtship before I fell so hard in love with her.

It is important for Black and Brown people, whether in Africa or the diaspora, to learn about each other. To learn about our different cultures and what connects us, as well as the history and movements of our diverse communities through time and across the world. It is in our collective best interest, the interest of the Global Majority.

Success will depend on our ability to create more unity and tackle the fight for racial equity, globally, as one.

The lies or convenient half-truths were popping up everywhere as I settled into my new American life. Watching television was another eye-opener to how much media played into molding the minds of people about a place and its inhabitants.

The questions we were getting about the continent from non-African fellow college students were fed by what they saw portrayed on TV. I realized this would also be true for children and be the foundation upon which they would build their cultural knowledge, or lack thereof, when it came to people from outside the United States of America.

The issue of misrepresentation was often discussed within our international students' circle, particularly among African students. I was not the only one bothered by the consequences of the prejudiced and misconstrued images of our homes and way of life as sold to American audiences.

I remember often watching documentaries, learning about some tribes for the first time myself and wondering how the film crew knew to go that deep to find them and why it was that they insisted on only showing those parts as what Africa looks like. I did get my answer later in that graduate school spat with the marketing executive at National Geographic.

For years, before and after that, it bothered me that this was massively pushed, and that so many consumed and were satisfied with that being the only image of Africa they had and operated from. It created a source of crazy questions coming at us from college students.

Among the friends I engaged on these issues, quite a bit was with two young men from Togo and Ghana. The former, Sly, worked as a DJ on the campus radio station and effectively used his platform to educate as much as he could and hosted talks with guests of all backgrounds. The second guy, Nana (God rest his young soul) worked with Sly at times, and they were both quite popular on campus.

In our talks, we realized that complaining or being petty about what we observed really would do nothing to change it.

We needed to be smart and strategic in drawing people in and making the challenge an opportunity to contribute to positive change.

And so, we teamed up and started a small venture aimed at taking the true image of Africa into Jacksonville schools where children would ask us questions and we could catch the misrepresentation early with proper answers. We called our project *Sankofa*, the Ghanaian Adinkra symbol that stood for 'Go back and fetch it' or return to your roots. This was a fulfilling experience and a fun one as well.

Our set up included a choreographed dance (that we performed together for attendees to watch), as well as question and answer sessions where kids and their teachers asked anything they wanted to know about Africa. After we introduced ourselves and told them a little bit about where we came from, there was a small party that Nana and Sly DJ'ed while I taught the kids some moves. We all had fun together to the beats of mama Africa. We did this in several elementary schools over a couple of semesters and it was always well received.

This experience taught me – the forever impatient young Taurus with strong petty vibes – to listen, be calm, and tolerant when answering even the most insane questions, because they were coming from children... and I couldn't get petty with the kids! I did, however, reveal to the little girl who excitedly asked if we saw lions everywhere in Africa that the first time I ever saw lions, elephants, and camels was at a circus in Paris; I couldn't help it.

The children were going at it with the questions, and this exercise required some major composure. A few kids wanted to know how one gets to Africa, while others wondered if there were houses or clothes available there.

While certain questions were cute like the ones about whether Simba (the Lion King) really lived in Africa, others required a poker face and slow breathing to deliver an even-toned answer.
The question on whether Africans ate little white children will always stick in my mind. That poor child was probably threatened at home, when he didn't stay in line, with a trip to cannibal land Africa to get devoured. He asked with the widest, fearful eyes and as I debunked the myth as nicely as possible, adding that he had been with us all day and the only food we were interested in was the lunch we shared. I realized I most likely just killed the overtly racist deterrent system the adults in that child's home had put in place.

I felt a deep sense of fulfillment and victory and the moment made the whole endeavor more worthy for me. In time and with experience, I would find other ways to debunk everyday comparative tactics used in the US to the detriment of Africa. Like telling kids who wouldn't eat their meals or finish their dinner that there were starving kids in Africa who didn't have what they had and so they shouldn't waste it.

Yes, they should not waste, but there really is no need to propel oneself all the way to Africa to find starving kids. There are plenty right there in the United States, much closer and more relatable to them, whose experiences can be a channel to teach kids about food insecurity and poverty and inspire them with the local community development work combating these issues.

But we insist on lying to them. We continue teaching children in history classes far and wide that Christopher Columbus *discovered* America or keeping them in an unrealistic bubble of *perfection* by mirroring to them a problem-free USA versus a problem-filled rest of the world. This benefits no one, much less the fostering of equitable and respectful relationships across this world.

I had many tense debates in college, mainly in international economics classes, with US Marines and other white American students who would say the craziest things. They were left to my wrath for an answer by our professor who understood by then that I was not to be played with when it came to negatively portraying Africa with empty prejudiced statements.

I will always remember my two infamous Marine colleagues in International Economics class and their antics calling anything non-American, uncivilized, and barbaric. I had a field day when the 2000 elections came around and the US was in that big Florida results debacle: I would ask them every class, "Hey guys, no president yet?" Because they would often use elections as an example of why their country was so much further ahead and more civilized than others.

I made it a point to tell them they were pitiful ambassadors if all they could report from their travels were judgements on other cultures. They obviously took no time to learn or understand, and their objective was to simply demonstrate that, as they often said in class, "America is the best country in the world". Says who? Based on what criteria?

That phrase was entirely rooted in ego, power, and white supremacy, and was shoved down children and adults' throats with nothing as proof other than a notion of superiority which then showed in their attitudes and behavior in and outside the USA. Maybe not so coincidentally, and to this day, too many generally white American tourists have a vile reputation around the world for being disrespectful and arrogant... no wonder why.

SAD 6: Learning *Service*
The beautiful nuggets

Moving to the US came with its share of cultural shock but there were also some amazing learning experiences along the way. The excitement I had about being in this new environment made me very open to new experiences and curious about how things worked.

I was always committed to learning from the US to be able to better contribute to my own country and continent's development and so here I was, ripe for the absorption! And I must say, the most fulfilling thing I learned in the US was the strong sense of service my undergraduate alma mater instilled in me.

As a Florida West Africa Linkage Institute (commonly called FLAWI) scholarship student there was an obligation to complete a certain number of community service hours each semester, so *service* started because I had to, but soon became a personal commitment and integral part of my life. I had no formal knowledge of volunteering prior to college, even though I had done community service countless times in high school and in my neighborhood, without it being called that. In fact, my older sister and I would head to the SOS Children's Village across from our house to play with the kids as a way to relieve the community moms. We also participated in the many street cleaning '*set setal*' events around our community, which back then were much more common than they are now, sadly.

Fulfilling my fifty hours of community service per semester to satisfy my scholarship's requirement meant discovering the student volunteer center. There I learned to consult the large manual with all the current opportunities and how they were classified in terms of interest and required time. I explored different ways to be a productive and engaged member of my community. Soon, I was joining the Volunteer Association and a host of other clubs and was participating in countless events from cleaning creeks to feeding the homeless.

I also applied and was selected to participate in the prestigious UNF Presidential Envoys, whose activities and hosting duties for university guests gave me even more chances to volunteer while meeting lots of inspiring people. Never did any of it feel like working for free because each event was a clear way to do something for the common interest and be remunerated by the pride and feel-good sensation that type of productivity brought.

In Senegal, there is a Wolof word *–ngorr–* which describes a mix of gratitude, dignity, self-esteem, and pride.

We say when someone does something for you, when you have the opportunity to repay in any way, show them they aren't built with more *ngorr* than you, as a show of gratitude. I took that to heart and decided that this country giving me a scholarship to fulfill my academic dreams would not have more *ngorr* than me, and *service* was where I saw the opportunity to demonstrate that.

In learning service, I also realized a key piece was missing and progressively worsening in my home country: this sense of 'doing' for our country. We also lost the sense of being responsible and proud. We must foster true patriotism and love for ourselves and our land.

Civic education was a staple when I was in middle school, and teachers told us about the constitution, our full national anthem's meanings, and key civic duties of a Senegalese. It instilled pride and respect for the country we were living in. This educational gem has now all but disappeared and the consequences are dire.

When my mother drove us to school as a child, we would pass in front of the Ministry of Interior (the equivalent of the Department of Home Affairs) right at the time the flag was being raised every morning and all the pedestrians and cars would stop. Some would place their right hand on their chest, and we would all watch our colors fly high at the top of the flagpole before we resumed our walk or drive; today this ceremony has lost its solemnity as many people driving or walking by do not even seem to notice, or worse, *know* the symbolic moment they are witnessing as they strut right on without stopping at all.

This is not to say that Civic Education is perfect in the US, far from it if we just consider the national anthem part. Those who have studied the entire Star-Spangled banner understand that the lesser-known parts are not warm and fuzzy, and contain racist lyrics that reflect its slave-owner author, Francis Scott Key.

Citizens are caught at the cradle with songs like *I know I can be what I wanna be* to build their belief that nothing is impossible and that has a huge psychological effort in instilling in them the notion that they live in 'the best country in the world'. These tactics simultaneously build deep patriotism and often wide ignorance and disdain towards anything non-American.

The balance of loving yourself and country while respecting that you are not alone or superior to all is missed. In turn, it can cause either a lack of interest in even recognizing and learning about other cultures, or a superiority complex accompanied with arrogance and belittling of foreigners. Of course, not all Americans are this way. Unfortunately, enough are to have created this reputation, which is not only seen in the US but with many tourists when they decide to venture out with this attitude.

There is also a stark dichotomy in this self-promotion and positioning of America (the US) as 'the best country in the world' and Americans as 'superior to all' with the way this same country has been treating its Black and Brown citizens.

It is as if 'American', in all these efforts, didn't mean 'Black or Brown'.

Because for the many who have fallen at the hands of police brutality, mass incarceration, redlining to name a few we will dive into later, the US is far from being 'the best country in the world'… in fact, it isn't even the safest.

For the sake of relating my positive experience with learning service here, I will keep these discoveries for a separate chapter about me finally meeting 'the System' and 'the Man'.

The famous John Fitzgerald Kennedy quote, "Ask not what your country can do for you but what you can do for your country" was something I saw strongly in my college experience and drew much inspiration from.

As I began my journey of volunteerism, I came to discover the community my alma mater belonged to and the various institutions therein: the homeless and women shelters, the elderly nursing homes, the community-based associations that did environmental activities like cleaning the river, etc. I enjoyed participating in activities with these different organizations because not only did it make me feel like I was a productive member of the community I now lived in, but it also taught me about the makeup of this society and gave me ideas on how to adapt similar processes in my own home country.

Tying volunteerism to certain factors like scholarships and making it a sure way to build one's resume before entering the professional world is a very effective strategy. Whether they were pointed events or actual volunteer positions such as heading student clubs or belonging to a formalized ambassador group like the Envoys, it was a valuable work experience.

Although I had a part-time job on campus, it was the volunteer hours I racked up along the way that taught me leadership skills and came in handy along my life journey. They helped demonstrate to me the importance of paying it forward. My volunteering was also a strong addition to my resume. It came in handy when I was looking for jobs or applying for academic opportunities.

My proudest moment as an international student was being selected as the recipient of the Class of 2000 Fall Commencement Senior Service Award, rewarding the student with the most volunteer hours and engagement. I wasn't volunteering with an award in mind. What made this the proudest moment is how it allowed me to yet again show *ngorr*, but this time towards my parents who had supported my undergraduate studies journey in Florida

74

alongside my scholarship grantor.

I told my father about the award before graduation day, and we decided to surprise my mom and sister by keeping it a secret from them until the ceremony. While the entire graduating class entered the arena first, the Senior Service Award and Caring Award recipients came afterwards, with the dignitaries' procession, and sat on the podium with the university president.

My dad told me that while the graduating class started to enter and fill the seats, my mom kept asking him where I was and why she couldn't see me, and whether I was late again like I often was in high school. Once everyone was in and they announced the presidential procession, my dad told her to look closely, and pointed at her daughter entering the arena with the university president's crew; my mother was overjoyed... That alone was worth every single minute of volunteering that afforded me this award because I made my community proud. Most importantly, I showed my mom that her fight for my dreams wasn't in vain (and my dad that my coming to the US bore fruit).

Service wasn't the only gem I learned along my American journey. I also became aware of what it is to be a consumer with rights and how to defend those rights. In college, my friends and I used to have this inside joke that the Americans were 'sue-happy', folks sued each other or companies for any and everything, and oftentimes won! However, we soon realized what that truly meant; there were such things as consumer protection and rights. This country had processes that everyone could follow to ensure their rights were protected.

If a medicine caused life-altering or threatening issues, it was recalled and ads from law firms would start flooding the TV and radio, calling on those who may have consumed it to band together in a lawsuit to get compensated for the damages the product had caused. If someone crashed into you and was at-fault, causing you material and physical damage, there was a process to ensure you were compensated for your losses. If a store made mistakes, or sold you expired stuff or defective items, there was a complaint process to ensure you got your money back and sometimes even more, whether monetary or not, as a customer service gesture of good faith.

These processes are a bit harder to find or draw benefits from in my home-country... some a lot harder, and that's something many of us deplore. I remember many times in the US where I called customer service or wrote a fiery letter to complain about an issue; one of those times to a car dealership headquarters. This letter was for the overt racism shown at their lot in Jacksonville FL where somehow the lot attendants would just sit and stare at the Black customers but jump up to help a white one, leaving the five (two couples and one individual) previously browsing people unattended.

As if the Black customers were not expected to afford the cars. The white couple left without buying anything, one Black couple purchased a vehicle, the other left angry, and the individual (me) left to buy the same car elsewhere. In the current age of social media, the letter would have been a damaging online post tagging their HQ and causing a firestorm. Back then, in the early 2000s, it generated an apology and offer for free services on the vehicle.

Regardless of what answer came back, the power of a customer in the US is relatively and exponentially better than in Senegal, where unfortunately customer service is often horrendous. It sadly makes the rare times you see impeccable service, which should be standard, some impressive moments to cherish.

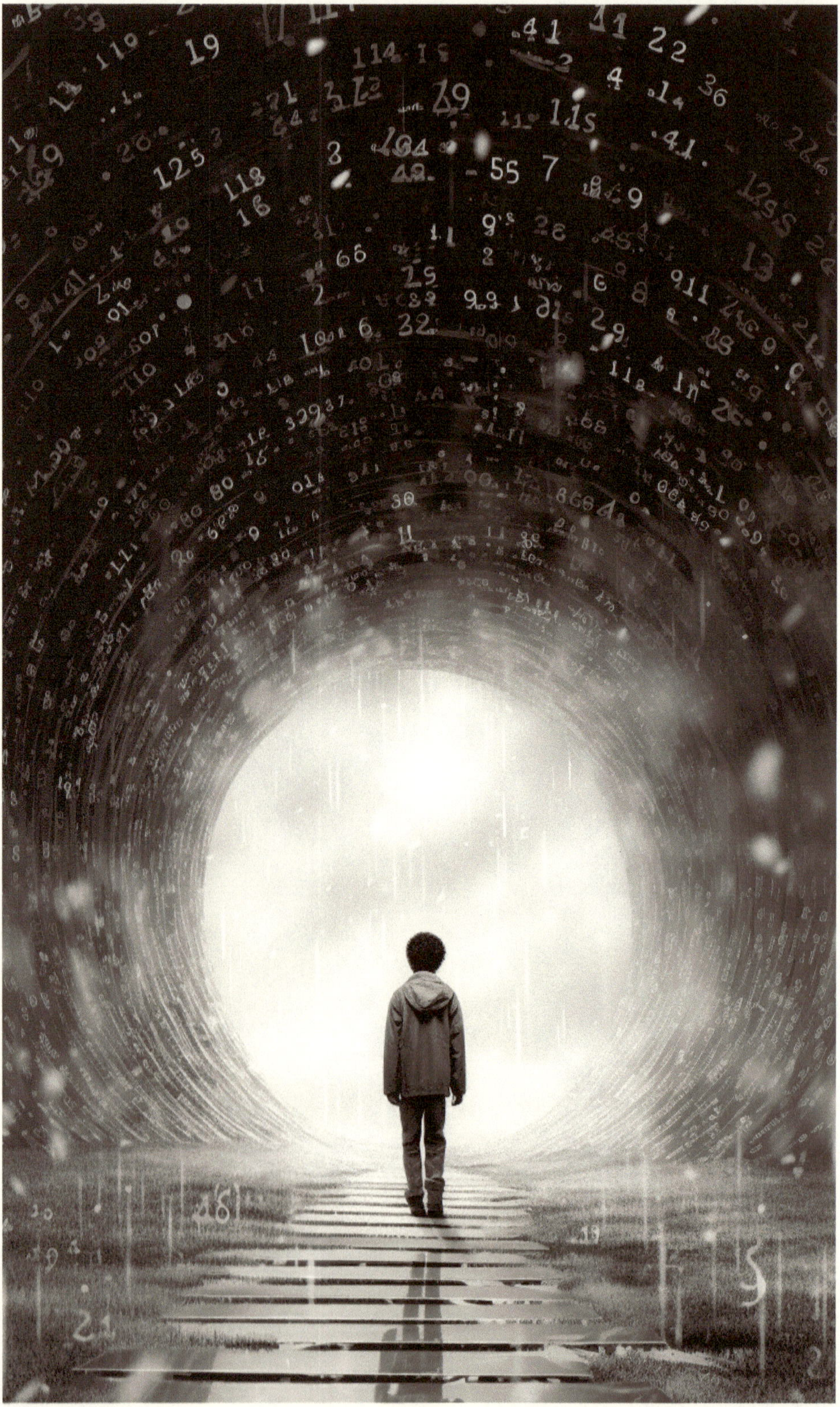

SAD 7: Becoming a Number

Renamed then redefined by a social security number, a credit score, and sometimes a whole new life story

One of the first stops you make as a new incoming student in the US is the infamous trip to get 'branded' at the Social Security office; I say branded because you do not realize, just like a cow approaching the hot iron, that the unique number you are about to be given is going to label you and your identity in that country.

Your social security number will be at the crux of many decisions that will completely stir, and sometimes doom your life. For me, the Social Security Office is also where, on a second visit later, I was given the suggestion to initial my 'first name' to fix the frustration of people being unable to pronounce it. I constantly had to explain that I go by Anta and always have and continuously correct the many types of butchering my name had to go through daily.

Somehow, I learned to say everyone's name properly, and Americans said they struggled with mine but easily pronounced Schwarzenegger… okay. The US is a country that doesn't really try to understand or include other cultures or cultural norms in its processes, despite being a melting pot of a country made up of people from far and wide.

The whole first, middle, last name thing was really rough on us African students. Many of us carried multiple names in our whole names, some had two surnames, some had names that they were not called by and the one they were called was not necessarily the first one… Here we were, asked to put our identities in preset boxes that did not always fit the bill. My name is Ndeye Anta, yet I was always Anta to everyone at home.

'Ndeye' means mom. Often, those named after one of their parents' moms would have a Ndeye before their name, or a 'Mame' if their namesake was a grandparent, or 'Pape' for a parents' dad. Sometimes, a child's namesake already had Ndeye or Mame in front of their name and that trickled down to the baby. But a Ndeye or Mame alone was rare. So, when I arrived and this became the norm to section my name into first, middle, last, I would struggle and be obligated to place Ndeye first then Anta in the middle. Just like that *boom!* my actual name, the one everyone knew me by, the one I grew up answering to, my name-name just disappeared!

Here everyone was calling me, or rather trying to call me, "Ndeye". They were pronouncing it all kinds of ways except the right way, prefacing or disclaiming their errors with all sorts of microaggressions. Oh, how hard or unusual this name was, snickering, acting impressed or surprised. Coming at it like they were about to compete in a decathlon, not even trying at all sometimes under the pretense that the name was just too hard for them... But you CAN say Schwarzenegger though.

Even with Anta, people found a way to act out. I will never forget the day the front desk person at a doctor's office in Florida actually added an 'i' to my already filled out forms, then called me Anita, and when I did not answer, she motioned to me. I told her it was not *Anita* but *Anta*, and she looked all puzzled, as if there just could be no way someone would NOT be called Anita with an 'i'... as if I did not know how to spell my own name.

Although many friends and relatives actually nicknamed me Anita back in Senegal, from that day forward, I radically refused to be called Anita and systematically corrected anyone who tried, forcing them to call me by my name Anta, not to be pronounced like *ant* either, because I had that, along with the spelling AntE more times than I can count.

Once I got the coveted social security number, then and only then was I able to open a bank account, fill out any relevant applications, and get my driver's license. But also, to fall for the predatory lending going on around campus by credit card companies. As an international student new to the US, I had no idea how a social security number worked.

I did not know that it was essentially the beginning of your brand as a consumer and would follow you forever. Neither had I ever had a credit card or any form of related financial education. So of course, for my three roommates and I, responding to the aggressive marketing of the credit card solicitors and their tables full of free goodies was more fun than well-thought out.

"Just fill out this simple application in exchange for a t-shirt, mug, small teddy bear, etc." – as they so trivially framed it – a no-brainer. And we filled out more than one, placing our freshly delivered social security numbers and signatures on several of these forms and proudly walking away with our free, oversized logo-branded t-shirts.

Well, a few weeks later, the mail arrived. With it came three brand new plastic cards with $100 and $200 limits, a thick stack of fine print none of us ever read, and multiple ensuing trips to the mall for shopping sprees we would sorely regret.

We later understood that the importance of establishing credit in the US was pretty much up there with breathing oxygen.

The credit history and score attached would be qualifiers and therefore define our lives in terms of financial ease or difficulty.

We were wide-eyed, first-time credit card holders, unbeknownst to our parents, and we had plastic money. Buying clothes, shoes, and makeup that we thought we could afford, when in fact we absolutely could not since we were also purchasing them with 17 to 24 percent added interest and would be repaying their cost for many months to come.

In fact, soon what came along in the mail were bills and we continued to fall for the scheme of only paying the minimum due, instead of the full amount when we had the money, essentially only covering a small portion of the principal due while forking out mostly interest.

Most of us stopped paying once we realized we were actually paying far more than what we had spent, not realizing the negative impact it would have on our credit history and score. We learned the hard way.

These rookie mistakes later came back to haunt me when looking to get a student loan for my graduate degree. But the crazy part is that building credit history seems to be forced in the US. I witnessed and lived in situations where deciding not to use credit and patiently saving for a big purchase was frowned upon. In fact, after understanding credit a lot more and realizing how defining it was, I went several years without using any of the paid-off credit cards I had, and also saving to buy anything I needed that was a big-ticket item.

In 2011, I was returning to the US from an 18-month professional stint in Senegal and needed to buy a new vehicle. I was rejected for credit by the first lender who said my credit history had too big of a hole, and my own credit union bank said the same thing in their original rejection later. However, I used those college-nurtured chops in consumer rights and did not take no for an answer. I called the bank and proceeded to explain why I had not used credit in a while and negotiated with the underwriter until she reversed her decision.

I was desperate to get a car, having recently moved to Atlanta for work, and my persistence paid off. However, this decision to try and stay away from consumerism on credit persistently came back to haunt me as my credit score kept tumbling despite me working a well-paid job and being able to afford what I needed in life.

In fact, years later, working in Rockville, MD, I wanted to purchase a condominium and get out of renting. I was making above the required income, had all the necessary paperwork, but was unable to get approved for a mortgage because my credit score was 22 points below the required minimum... the credit score (when I had been paying timely rent that was way higher than what the mortgage was going to be) was what sealed my fate and prevented me from homeownership that time around.

I was only able to make that purchase two years later, after working on reestablishing my credit and resuming a very calculated and strategic use of my credit cards. I would make a small purchase every month (one of my grocery trips, a shirt at the mall, a restaurant meal) and pay it right away online as soon as it showed up on my transaction list.

I also made use of the free financial advisor services at my banks and spoke to professionals for advice on how to efficiently save for a down payment. It involved a lot of research on various programs available to first-time homeowners and although I did not use one, it truly elevated my knowledge and awareness of opportunities and strategies to better prepare for purchasing a home.

How is one supposed to know all this fresh from a plane into a country where the whole consumer finance system rests on credit history and scores and decisions made often without much context to the detriment of so many people and communities

They too had fallen into this trap as youngsters and could not escape the claws of a punitive credit system when the time came to light the house or to get a phone, a car, or other products or services.

Most Americans did not have a rich parent who could just give them a wad of cash to purchase a big-ticket item like a car or a house. I had several Black friends along the way who explained that as a child, their parents had to use their kids' social security numbers to secure utility accounts.

There were also stories of parents who used a child's social security number to open credit lines and use them for mundane things. That kid would later find huge debts on their credit file they never generated themselves but were left to clean up.

Either way, these experiences showed me the importance of financial literacy and education as it can help those who are most vulnerable to these factors be better prepared. I suppose the benefits of the linked social security number and credit systems outweigh the disadvantages, given how efficiently it allows many areas of the country to run.

The experience can definitely be traumatic and detrimental to many under-resourced people and communities.

As an African immigrant, it wasn't just becoming a 9-digit code and a credit score that was unusual, it was also automatically being the main character in some poverty sap story. Somehow, it seemed to fit us best, or make us more exotic and digestible to our white counterparts. And sometimes this extended to African Americans as well. There are so many examples of this in my journey that they could fit into their own book, but let's explore two of them here, both happened a few years apart in Florida.

The first took place in the mostly white neighborhood I lived in when I reluctantly returned to Jacksonville for work after graduating with my master's in Washington, DC.

My then boyfriend (and soon-to-be husband) of almost five years lived there, and we were going to only start out temporarily living in Florida and then seek a city with more international opportunities. None of that ever happened and that ultimately doomed our marriage but that's another story!

As a young married couple, we lived in a quaint little neighborhood where we were one of two Black families on our whole street and several blocks.

A few houses down from us lived an old white man, he must have been in his late seventies or early eighties. So, this man lived through the segregation period. We would pass him often driving out of the neighborhood and we would wave, or wave back but never really engaged him much more than that.

One day, on our way out, he hailed us down. As we stopped the car, he walked up to the driver's window, holding on to his cane, frail on his legs. We rolled the window down and exchanged hellos, then he addressed my then-husband pointing to a Cadillac parked on his driveway with a 'for sale' sign on it, and said: "Son, might you know one of your Black brothers who would be interested in buying this car? I know how y'all like these Cadillacs!"

My ex-husband was way more diplomatic than me, and while I had already made up my mind that our neighbor was racist and ridiculous, he showed more patience and responded to the old man nicely, saying he didn't but would keep it in mind. The man then shifted his focus to me, and said he noticed an accent when I responded to his initial greetings and wanted to know where I was from, not before wildly guessing Jamaica. I replied that I was from Senegal, West Africa.

This man almost immediately said: "Ooooh, did your father come to this country to get a better life?" I was completely dumbfounded, and I felt my ex-husband's hand on mine as if he knew I was about to lose my cool and was trying to calm me down.

I looked at our neighbor and smiled before saying to him that my father was actually living his best retirement life back home after a long successful career in the airline industry and that I wasn't in the US because I was running away from any misery but rather in search for higher education. I added that in fact I had just moved back to Jacksonville after successfully graduating from The George Washington University in the nation's capital.

He widened his eyes, then started formulating some type of congratulations punctuated with the ever so micro aggressive, "You are so articulate."

My ex-husband didn't give me time to respond, he quickly said thanks, rolled the window up, and drove off. I was livid. We spoke about the nerve and probable racist vantage point we just encountered the rest of the day and in many conversations, we had afterward.

My then-husband was gardening one early morning a few years later when this same old man fell outside his home. He ran and helped him up. He called an ambulance and stayed with him until they arrived.

Even on that day, when attempting to show gratitude in front of the emergency medical team, the man pointed out his race when referring to my ex-husband as "his Black neighbor" … as if it wasn't already obvious, but clearly that was a qualifier of importance for him.

Another notable instance when somebody tried to make me an automatic sap story happened almost ten years later, when I was working on an arts and culture project while on sabbatical. I had traveled back to Jacksonville to explore some partnerships as the project had been selected to participate in a pitch contest in Berlin. The selection caught my Alma mater's attention. A young journalism student was deployed to write about it for a local newspaper. She contacted me and I sent her information about the project along with a standard biography.

When she sent me her draft article to review, a sentence jumped out in the section where she was describing me; "Despite her humble beginnings in Senegal…" even though nowhere in my biography or the call we had did I mention any such background.

Disbelief came over me as I stood there running through our conversations in my head, re-reading my own biography, wondering where this young white girl could have gotten this information or impression from. Nowhere! She got it from nowhere, other than her own mind. Likely the same image that many of my fellow students had when I was in college; those who were asking me whether I lived under trees or had clothes back in big wild Africa.

I called and asked her to remove that sentence. Although, I explained, it is endearing to present the story as that young African girl who overcame dire straits and hard life and whose project was one of the 25 out of 200 selected worldwide to pitch in Berlin, I didn't want to be mis-portrayed and end up appearing as a fraud.

Humble beginnings hardly described my private school education and BMW ride each morning to my downtown Catholic school with my mom and siblings. My parents were not filthy rich, but they worked hard to provide us with a comfortable life, and it was definitely not matching this poverty childhood she had somehow felt necessary to give me to make my story more appealing.

I guess it really was difficult to envision a young African child as anything other than starving, poor, and needy; just like the many infomercials shown on TV at the time, followed by the oh so necessary white-savior 1-800-number to call to ease their misery with a donation.

SAD 8: The *System* and The *Man* are Real

Discovering the true face of America

My career in public health is truly what started peeling back the layers of the US *system* for me and exposing the institutional racism upon which it was founded.

Upon returning to Jacksonville, FL after my Master's program I got my first job at a research institute running a health literacy study focused on diabetes and hypertension. My work was based in the two zip codes hardest hit by chronic diseases and poor health outcomes, an area with nearly 80% African American residents and largely categorized as low-income.

I taught classes for a group of Black doctors' patients who had uncontrolled diabetes and hypertension and were all also Black. These classes included nutrition sessions and those were really interesting because here I was, a young woman fresh out of school trying to teach grandmothers how to cook their soul food... It was really funny at times!

They did not hold back on the side eyes when I attempted to convince them to use substitutions for their most prized family recipes. I loved talking to them and understanding their habits and the classes often ended late because we took time to have conversations and get to know each other. We really enjoyed the time spent together. This led me to start asking questions, when I saw that many of the folks in class were now aware of the information and recommendations, but still their numbers remained high or sometimes kept rising.

I began understanding what social determinants of health were all about through the answers I would get from the participants. Some told me they knew they needed fruits and vegetables, but they had no supermarket selling fresh options for miles or public transportation took too long. Others explained that what they could get from a dollar menu at one of the many fast foods around them provided more quantity to feed their family. Their sharing also revealed they had to choose between paying a bill and purchasing insulin or other medicine. They also struggled with being uninsured or underinsured.

It wasn't long before I started realizing that you could teach people how to eat all you wanted, but if they didn't have access to the food they needed, what was the use of such information? The class also had questions about the content of the education provided. African Americans were among the populations most at risk for type two diabetes and hypertension, alongside most non-white populations. .

The class wanted to know why, especially since Caucasians were at significantly less risk. At the time, I didn't have an answer and that bothered me. This prompted a long, studious, heart wrenching journey to uncover a history of institutional racism and its devastating effects on public health. What I learned from the patients in my class already gave me an inkling that what I was doing, albeit useful, was not nearly enough if the objective was to allow people to control their chronic disease successfully and sustainably.

When an opportunity came up a couple of years later to lead the flagship diabetes disparities reduction program at the local health department, I jumped on it and was hired to join one of the best teams I have ever worked with, both in terms of expertise and humanism. This is the workplace where I made real friends and we truly worked in symbiosis toward objectives we knew were beyond health and about more than individual patients.

The program had community health workers, and we quickly developed a way to ensure they were positioned as true community liaisons, sharing information that connected populations to the very things they explained were inaccessible: healthcare, proper insurance, farmer's markets within their reach, etc. We also successfully integrated cooking demos within our classes with most of the go-to recipes they had been eating for decades that had family and traditional significance. But used variations that didn't sacrifice taste for health.

It was a hit, and our program often quadrupled its objectives. During these years with the health department, I spent lots of time volunteering in the community and interacting with the same people we were reaching in our programs. My demonstration of *ngorr* did not stop when I graduated college; I continued to offer my time as long as I was a member of this community and country. I also continued to pursue my desire to work in international development by doing what I could through community development in the US.

This precious time greatly contributed to my own educational journey about the history of my adopted country, and the struggles of Black America. I saw the link between the quality of schools and what people designated as less than desirable neighborhoods: schools got a large part of funding from property taxes which were higher in 'richer' (understand whiter) neighborhoods and thus the 'good schools' were in high-tax areas.

Since schools were assigned, if you wanted your kids in a good school, you either moved (and good luck affording those areas if your income wasn't high enough), or you put them in private school, or you lied about where your address was, at the risk of being sent to jail (yes, it has happened more than once) for wanting better for your children.

I witnessed gentrification, as formerly known as 'less desirable' neighborhoods became attractive to white folks for some reason or another, and they began to move in, buying up and renovating properties that sold for higher prices, progressively raising the value and property taxes of whole areas, driving out low-income families (understand Black and Brown), and ultimately taking over.

I will always remember the shocking change in Harlem, NY between my first visit on vacation in the early nineties, subsequent visits in my early college years in the late nineties where the metro pretty much only saw flows of Black and Brown people getting in and out between 116th and 125th Street, compared to the visits in 2015 where I saw white girls jogging with their dogs right there on Malcolm X Avenue. That was a completely different vibe!

A good friend of mine explained that rental discrimination was also happening in Harlem, and that she had been a victim of it herself. The rental agent she had been speaking to and emailing for weeks to get an apartment finally got her to the last step of approval only to ghost my friend once she invited her into the office and found out the applicant was Black and not "…from Paris or something with that beautiful, rare name and that perfect English."

'The System' was like an onion, the more you peeled, the more layers you saw and the more susceptible you were to cry.

Throughout my public health career, I was confronted with many of the root causes of health inequities: food insecurity, housing insecurity, poverty, lack of access to basic needs, just to name a few. As I peeled the layers of this onion, it became clear that the foundation of these root causes was racism. By the time I had left Florida to work on policy, systems and environmental changes in Atlanta and DC, I had a clear idea of what 'the System' and who 'the Man' were… a collective set of oppressive factors and people whose sole reason for existing was to keep the power dynamics in favor of white people and manage non-whites in a controllable environment where this status quo will not be dismantled.

As Ava Duvernay skillfully exposed in her notorious documentaries *13th* (amendment) and *When They See Us*, Jim Crow has never truly been abolished in the US. It just moves through, changing clothes to protect the reign of white supremacy.

It is unbelievable that in the 2022 local elections in the USA, slavery was on the ballot for five states, leading Alabama, Tennessee, and Vermont to approve measures to amend their state constitutions in order to prohibit the use of slavery and involuntary servitude as a punishment for crimes. In modern times, that would mean prison labor could be scaled back in those states.

As a reminder, before the November 2022 elections, there were still nineteen states in the USA with constitutions that openly allowed slavery, involuntary servitude, or both as legal punishments for a crime…

Slavery was kept alive by enacting mass incarceration in the USA (dubbed the New Jim Crow by attorney and author, Michelle Alexander in her acclaimed 2010 bestseller), targeting Black and Brown people to keep fueling the free and forced labor. 'The Man', or collective hands holding the power of decisions in the executive, legislative, and judicial processes of the land, ensured 'the System' was maintained and those that insist on qualifying the latter as broken just don't realize or fathom that it is in fact working exactly as it was intended to work.

When the Founding Fathers gathered to draw the constitution of the United States of America and began with "We the People…", they didn't mean Black and Brown folk.

Back then, we were not valued as a full person; thus, to meaningfully reform 'the System', it will require dismantlement and reconstruction with the context and intention where "We the People" refers to each and every one equitably, and those that were knowingly ignored for the first few centuries should be compensated for it.

My beloved America, who had lured, pulled, and caught me in her arms of illusions, was slowly starting to suffocate my dream by showing a side to her I had never suspected was this deep and cruel.

She began chipping at my heart over the years by propelling me one step forward and multiple steps back in a roller coaster of experience and emotions that kept me in the limbo of a love-hate relationship with her.

On one hand, I had a successful academic and professional career that allowed me to support myself and navigate through jobs that taught me a lot. On the other hand, I was moving through a system where I often experienced racism subtle enough to be difficult to prove but aggressive enough to know what it was.

I have been in jobs where I was passed up for promotions that were given to the white girl who produced zero results but was an ace at networking and kissing up to the often starkly white leadership. So many times, I have heard about how I needed to go back to Africa if I wasn't happy with the way America worked a million times, often from poor white people who were more forward with their racism because white privilege doesn't only benefit wealthy whites.

Yes, it was a roller coaster of highs and lows. I benefited from a permanent resident status that I was happy to keep until I saw Barack Obama win the presidency in 2008, which convinced me to apply for citizenship and fully support him going forward with my work and right to vote. This also always gave me the power of options, which most of my fellow home-country men and women do not always have in terms of where they want to live and take their family.

Twice, I attempted to move back to Senegal before permanently doing so in 2019. My first time in 2010 lasted eighteen months before returning to the US because my desire to work in public health there was met with a system of nepotism and needing to know people to get a job in certain areas.

My second time was on sabbatical between 2014 and 2015, but I was going back and forth between the US and Senegal and that was the beauty of having options. So, the US definitely gave me a lot, and I kept my *ngorr* towards her throughout my journey.

However, on February 26, 2012, came the day she obliterated my heart, broke it in a million pieces and it would never really be the same ever again. 17-year-old Trayvon Martin was killed by George Zimmerman in Sanford Florida as he returned from the corner store with his candy and drink. His killer decided this kid looked threatening enough that he needed to confront him and ultimately kill him. Trayvon was wearing a hoodie at the time he was executed. Hoodies became synonymous with racial profiling and race-based killing aka lynching. The hoodie became a symbol to shed light on racism.

This particular event and the ensuing trial and acquittal of the perpetrator, his defiance, and the way he gathered supporters completely nauseated and broke me. I remember falling to the floor of my Atlanta condo, uncontrollably crying when the acquittal verdict fell. In utter shock and disbelief, staring at my TV screen, as if I were looking dead into the eyes of America who just stabbed me in the heart with a smile on her face saying "gotcha!"

The environment and discourse surrounding the Trayvon Martin killing was difficult to witness and hear. As the scenario kept repeating, my beloved's face became more and more evil and her racism and hate for Black and Brown people more and more evident:

Black Lives did not seem to matter, and I was a Black life.

The police also became an institution we had to protect ourselves from as the names of Black people of all ages murdered by police officers while just *being* kept coming:

- Eric Garner's breath was taken for suspicion of selling cigarettes;
- Tamir Rice was just being a 12-year-old boy playing with a toy gun at the park and fragile white gaze decided he was a grown man brandishing an arm and shot him dead;
- Walter Scott received five gunshots in the back after a traffic stop for running away;
- Alton Sterling was killed by police responding to a disturbance call outside a shop;
- Philando Castille was killed while driving with his girlfriend during a traffic stop where he reached for his license;
- Stephon Clark was shot seven times in his grandma's backyard.

The list went on even after my permanent departure from the USA. All of these people were unarmed, but interestingly the same police arrested white shooters several times and found a way to keep those armed and dangerous criminals alive and even well catered to for some. They bought a hamburger meal for 21-year-old Dylann Roof about sixteen hours after he was arrested for shooting nine people in a church in Charleston, South Carolina.

My heartbreak and spiritual journey, heightened by my 2012 pilgrimage to Mecca, led to my decision to take a sabbatical in mid-2013, as I needed to get away and center myself in the midst of all the emotions I was feeling. By then, I had been the victim of lots of Islamophobia in Georgia. This ranged from dirty looks to straight up questioning or insults from people I didn't know but who were triggered and bothered by the fact that I wore a scarf on my head (by choice) and thus was an obvious Muslim hijabi.

The time away took me to Oman, Senegal, giving me time to work on various consulting gigs and also my own arts-related project that was featured in a pitch festival in Berlin in 2014. Most importantly, it gave me the time to see what better preparation I needed if I wanted to move back to Africa permanently. That readiness was not just about degrees and professional competence. It, in fact, required psychological and social skills that the hybrid nature of having lived outside my home country for longer than I had in it rendered critical to acquire.

After my sabbatical, the power of options allowed me to return to the US and reintegrate my public health career. I was unhappily remarried, and pregnant when my then-employer hired me. Not facing discrimination while being with child was great, but I had a rough and short maternity leave.

The US is one of only six countries in the world where a national policy for paid parental leave does not exist.

Women have to apply for short-term disability and that is six to eight weeks maximum based on natural versus Cesarean birth; anything above and beyond that needs to have been accrued in paid time off. There is a lot to unpack here.

First of all, pregnancy is not a disability, and should have a policy granting proper leave for parents who have welcomed a child, whether biologically or via adoption. Secondly, while the USA is one of the few countries in the world without such a policy, it is the only one out of thirty-eight members of the Organization for Economic Cooperation and Development (OECD) without paid family leave. [source: https://bipartisanpolicy.org/explainer/paid-family-leave-across-oecd-countries/]

For a country considered a top economic power, that is quite shameful and shows an utter lack of leadership and inconsideration for working parents and their value. Being quite new at my job, I did not accrue enough leave to take more than what the short-term disability afforded me plus a couple of weeks, including one gifted by a coworker. I was back at work a mere two months after giving birth to my daughter and she was in daycare.

I remember traveling for work in my eighth month of pregnancy, then again with my daughter to a workshop when she was barely four months. I was an exclusively breastfeeding mother, struggling between the pumping schedule and the excruciating pain of not being able to when I had back-to-back meetings or long ones that ran into the timetable.

It was rough being a new mom in the US working world.

It was not made for us to win and somehow you felt that pressure and worked even harder to prove you were still sharp… all while still healing from physically making a human being for forty weeks, birthing then breastfeeding the child, being sleep deprived and constantly tired. But I was never one to back down from a challenge. I still pushed through, attaining incredible results, bringing innovation to my job, and constantly advocating for equity both in and outside work.

This didn't come without a cost. My daughter went to bed between 6.30 and 7.00 p.m. every night after I sleep trained her and she kept that schedule for a long time like clockwork. I would love to say this was done purely as a parenting tool, but I would be lying. I did it successfully, in large part, because of the professional pressure that had me coming home with my computer and the need for more time to work. Maybe I would have been kinder to myself if I didn't feel that intense need to prove that being a new mom did not decrease my competence, but the sad part is that I needed to prove that at all.

The pressure was more intense as a Black woman because I could not afford to try and find out what would happen if I slipped and became less sharp despite my situation.

I had been in too many professional environments where the intensity of the same mistake increased based on your skin color, or where you had to give exponentially more than your white counterpart to be recognized, while they were sailing through promotions that were undeserved. And so, I pressed on…

My work in public health progressively morphed as its focus became social justice and community development, which was an intersection of the multi-sectorial nature of population health and the need to be upstreamists if we wanted to achieve sustainable change for all.

Through this work, I would often use the analogy of the *River of health,* a popular concept among public health practitioners with diverse versions to explain the different levels of the Impact pyramid made popular by former Centers for Disease Control and Prevention Director, Thomas Frieden [www.tomfriedenpublichealth.net].

I adopted the United Way's version called *The Ogre Story*, which I came to adapt and use as a foundation to build upon in the trainings and talks I would give on the subject of health impact and social determinants of health.

The Ogre Story goes something like this:

One morning, villagers who lived by a river woke up to baby cries coming from the riverbanks. They rushed to the river and found a bunch of babies struggling in the water. Of course, several of the villagers jumped in the water and started extracting the babies but more babies kept coming downstream. Someone suggested moving mid-way up and extracting from that point so that the villagers downstream wouldn't be so overwhelmed; and so, a bunch of them did. They were able to get some of the babies out before they reached downstream, but still many passed them and ended up at the bottom, still overwhelming the villagers. Someone finally looked at the scene and asked: "but WHERE are all these babies coming from to begin with?!?" That villager proceeded way upstream at the source and found a huge ogre there tossing babies in the river. The real problem was the ogre and that's what needed to be neutralized to ensure no babies were found struggling downstream in the water.

In this story, the scene downstream represented caring for the already sick with interventions such as education and counseling, and clinical interventions, like medicine for diabetes and hypertension. The mid-streamers applied some level of prevention like long-term protective interventions such as vaccines, or more impactful context changes to make *the healthy choice the easy choice* such as fluoridation of water or cigarette taxes.

The upstreamists, however, would uncover, then tackle the very deepest root causes of negative or poor health outcomes which are harder to solve but carry the highest impact on population health: these are socio-economic factors like poverty, education, housing, and inequality. In other words, 'the System', and it would seem as if that ogre was no other than 'the Man'!

In my own adaptation of the story, I would always highlight the need for a multi-sectorial approach to population health that required the villager who went upstream and discovered the ogre to analyze him before returning to the village to gather a coalition with villagers of different skills and assets that could band together and take down the ogre/*Man*.

It was also important to highlight that the ogre/*Man* was standing on a solid foundation. One that gave him the energy to regenerate if the only thing the coalition targeted was the socio-economic factors that made up 'the System'. In fact, the ogre/*Man* was supported by racism and that was the cornerstone that allowed him to continue. Until we dismantled that foundation he was firmly standing on, he would keep coming back every time we found a solution for one of the aforementioned factors.

Being able to highlight the issues of population health and their intersectionality with institutional racism and community development was always effective because the power of storytelling is universal and reaches audiences of various backgrounds, education levels, ages, and experience. And the more I expanded my own education on these socio-economic factors and the history of racism that fueled their dysfunction for many people of the global majority that the US calls minority populations, the more I discovered just how deeply racist my beloved America was.

Several colleagues, professional partners, and authors are responsible for imparting important expertise and knowledge onto me throughout my career. I can never thank them enough for opening my eyes and keeping me unsheltered because it made me an unapologetic activist for social justice.

The birth of my daughter in 2016 was in the midst of the run for the US Presidential elections. I spent my whole pregnancy watching Donald Trump and his Make America Great Again (MAGA) gang run wild on TV, saying the craziest things, and in fact doing nothing else but Making Racism Win Again.

Somehow, I was much less in shock than most of my friends in the DC area for having heard that rhetoric time and again in Florida for years on end. I told them I had a feeling Trump was going to win and everyone said I was insane.

Two of my childhood friends came to visit me when I had my daughter in June. We were talking politics when I declared Trump was going to win the elections despite my profound opposition to him and his antics: they looked at me, and one of them, concerned, asked if I had postpartum depression.

I did not; I just knew that the America I had discovered over the years was filled to the brim with people who had been waiting their whole lives for someone to say out loud what they were thinking inside. They were waiting for someone on a leadership stage to validate their innermost racist sentiments and embolden them to follow suit without the risk of being ostracized or deemed politically incorrect… and oh, did they get emboldened.

Trump made racism okay and created monsters around him who, still mad about having had eight years of a Black president, were ready to do whatever it took to restore white supremacy, as if it ever left. The same way new voters came out in droves for Obama, new ones did for Trump.

Voters who were finally hearing what they felt, the sentiment that in order for America to be glorious, it had to be AmeriKKKa and its citizens who didn't look like them were not valid, valued, or respected. But make no mistake, these were not the only ones who voted for Trump.

I am convinced to this day that many who around the water cooler were claiming to be liberals and allies of BIPOC, in the secrecy of the voting booth stayed loyal to their deep actual feelings of superiority, or their skewed religious beliefs on which Trump played to garner the support of conservatives all of hues and backgrounds, despite being himself far from holy.

I am a Black, foreign-born, Muslim woman. I was everything MAGA loved to hate, and I increasingly felt unsafe and unwelcome in the US.

When Donald Trump was announced as the winner of the 2016 elections, I wasn't the least bit surprised, but I was greatly concerned. I knew we were in for a gloomy few years ahead, and every weird bit of news that plundered his first term after that was just another confirmation of this worry being valid.

My US citizenship didn't feel like a shield for any of it or protection for what could be... I felt like a walking target. I felt that under Trump's administration, even my citizenship as a naturalized American could be at risk. That time cohabitating with Trump and his supporters in the US leading to his election of 2016 and his first term was a time of anxiety and insecurity. My beloved America had taken on its full abusive role in our relationship.

I felt her weight on my heart, mind, and soul. I no longer felt her open arms hold me in comfort but rather squeeze me so tight I suffocated.

I was afraid for myself and for my daughter's future. I wanted out.

SAD 9: "The Hate U Give Little Infants Fucks Everybody"

- Tupac

Breaking Up with America and Extracting My Child from her Birthplace

The coup de grace in my decision to break up with America came when I lost my mother, suddenly, in 2018. She got sick that summer, but never did I imagine she was going to die… she passed at age sixty-eight, a week before her birthday and we were not ready…

I was not ready; my daughter was only two and a half and I did not want her to grow up without a maternal grandmother. I was so close to my maternal grandmother that when she passed away in 2001, it took me seven years to set foot back in Senegal in an unhealthy way to keep her alive in my mind. And even then, I was never able to go to her grave until my mom passed seventeen years after my grandmother's transition. I always say that my mother gave me a last gift when she passed away, and that was the courage to visit my grandma's tomb and finally come to grips with the fact that she was no longer of this world.

My mother's death hit me like a ton of bricks. I found out her illness was actually a terminal phase of cancer and lost her all in the span of four days… Her mom passed at age eighty-six and her grandmother lived way past a hundred.

So, I never expected my mom would not be around to see my daughter grow up and become a full-blown adult. I never expected my mom would leave before I completed all the intentions I had for her, all the trips I wanted us to take together, all the surprises and gifts I wanted to shower her with… I wasn't ready. I am still not ready. I wasn't done showing her the fruits of her hard labor and support for me.

I was numb for a long time, and today, nearly five years later, I still have days where the pain burns as if it were brand new. Days where I feel empty because by leaving, she also took a part of my reason for fighting through life.

But I thank God that the other reason is near and often is the one that senses my devastation and consoles me; I thank God for my daughter Aasiyah. She is wise beyond her years, and I somehow feel like a big part of my mother and grandmother lives in her, and that feeling warms my heart. When I found out my mom had passed, I was traveling for work in New Orleans.

I had already decided with my older sister who lived in Miami at the time that we would both go home to Senegal. The plan was to see our mother as I had just found out about the terminal nature of her illness, but we didn't have a clear prognosis on how much time she had left.

That conversation happened on a Saturday; my sister was leaving that Wednesday and I was leaving Saturday right after coming back from my work trip.

My mother didn't wait for us; she went peacefully on Tuesday October 9th. She must have known we would not stand to see her looking frail and emaciated and wanted us to keep the image of our vibrant energetic Mama when we thought of her. I shifted my ticket, and my sister and I arrived in Senegal after the burial, and all we had was a grave to pay our respects to…

Our dear Mama, who had been everything to us, who had always supported us and loved us unconditionally, our dear Mama who fervently prayed for us in a way that gave us wings and erased our every fear… our dear Mama was gone. I reverted to unhealthy mourning automatically by throwing myself into work after getting back to my job in the US ten days later.

I thought keeping myself busy would help, but my poor coping skills must have shown because a coworker who was not my direct supervisor, but on that level, called me into her office and asked me how I was doing. I replied I was okay, just busy.

She looked at me and said: "Anta, you just lost your mom and it's okay to not be okay; how can I support you so you can get home and be in the environment and the head space to properly mourn your mother?"

This moment in my professional life is the one that has touched me the most in terms of support. This leader saw what I was attempting to hide, and proactively sought to ensure I had what I needed. Something that included going with me through all the HR options and hoops so I could take generous time off, work out an intermittent remote work schedule, and benefit from true work life balance, not just one written everywhere but real nowhere.

I will forever be grateful to her empathy and her elevated sense of leadership. My daughter and I went home for about two months, and I knew right then that it was time to make concrete steps toward finding my way back permanently. My mom's dream was for me to come back to Senegal, and I was going to make that a building block .

Even before I had the chance to spend that important reflective time back home close to her resting place, another major block fell heavily atop my stash. It was so deep and heavy that I knew the breakup with America was final and all that was left was for me to grab my stuff and slam the door in her face, rebuking her back to *friend zone*. We could no longer be together after that episode because now she was gonna mess with my child.

In the few weeks between my mom's funeral and the time I got off to return to Senegal, I went to the movies alone to watch *The Hate U Give*. I used to love going to the movies, and for a long time I did, either alone or with friends. Then the mass shootings, including in houses of worship and movies started to unconsciously affect me. I began to feel anxious instead of enjoying my time in the theaters. I would often watch the exit doors when I was inside the theater.

Every time someone stood up during the film, I would secretly feel nervous and start running drills in my head in case this was a shooting waiting to happen.

It was exhausting and started happening not just at movie theaters but anywhere a crowd would gather, and this paranoia was taxing to say the least.

On this day, I was already feeling low and sad, so my mood wasn't at its best. I started watching the movie, and I could feel myself getting angry as my whole drama with America was literally playing out in front of me, showing me those devastating sides I had been uncovering over the years and putting it in the very real context of a Black family's lived experience.

Then it happened, the scene where the parents sat their two children down to have *the talk*. Except this was not about sexual education, it was about how they should act if they ever got pulled over by the police and wanted to stay alive. This talk was pretty much about how being Black could be the determining factor during a police arrest and result in their death if they made the 'wrong' move or had the inadequate attitude… I was hot!

It was not because I was unaware of what I was hearing, it was because I realized right then and there that if I chose to stay in the US, I would one day have to have this type of talk with my own chocolate drop of a daughter, who was already such a happy and sensitive child.

I would have to tell her that her beautiful brown skin was in fact dangerous to her very life in her own birth country.

After working so hard to instill in her a sense of Black pride and self-love all based on that same skin and heritage, I was absolutely *not* going to have that talk with her. I left that movie knowing I did not have the right to deprive Aasiyah of the same opportunity I had to live in an environment where everyone looked like me, where I never felt like a minority or endangered by a bullet, where I was always hyped up with tales of warrior ancestors and royal bloodlines.

I knew I had to choose whether I would engage that talk of police brutality as a warning in a context she would walk into daily, or a preparation within an enabling environment that would not bury her worth outside while I built it inside the home. I did not want her to be the infant to which society was giving hate. I didn't want her to grow up damaged with a f**k everybody

106

mentality, starting with herself. I couldn't fathom her suffering from the consequences of mental trauma, low self-esteem, anger, confusion about belonging, or whatever other destruction hate breeds.

I refused that life for this little girl I was already giving Patrice Lumumba parts in her beautiful thick hair. This little girl to whom I was reading the epic of Soundiata Keita as a bedtime story when she was just eight months old. My little girl who successfully chose the Black doll, the doll that looks like her, as the most beautiful in a doll test (readapted from the well-known Drs. Kenneth and Mamie Clark doll experiment). She raised her small fist in a Black power sign and screamed « me! » when I asked her who was going to change the world. My Aasiyah was not going to be treated as anything other than great, and I knew for that to happen, I had to make sure she didn't start school anywhere that would not authentically teach her about her true history.

So, I looked for jobs, focusing on three countries in Africa and selected one in Senegal. I left the United States of America to reside back on the African continent on September 15th, 2019, and have been in Senegal since. My daughter has flourished and is living her best life. I chose to extract us from her birthplace and my adopted country, breaking up with my childhood love, because I chose self-love and self-worth.

I realized America only loves the white supremacist reflection of herself and if you don't understand it fast enough, she will consume you and feed off your embers to keep her light projecting the so-called land of the free and home of the brave facade.

She will attract more lovers. She will fool those that fell for the belief that "We the People..." meant everyone and that the American Dream did not see color. She will fool them into thinking her arms around them are an embrace rather than a knee on their necks waiting to choke them into oppression.

December 2000 – University of North Florida Commencement with my Senior Service Award surrounded by my older sister Awa, my mother on the left, and my father on the right.

My mom and sister have both passed on, in 2018 and 2021 respectively. May their abode be with our Almighty God in Heaven.

Amen.

Dear United States of America,

I will always love you for what you have given me, what you have taught me, the people you have put in my life, and the expertise and competence I have gathered with you to fuel my career and life projects. However, I will not tolerate that to you my life doesn't matter, or that the life of my child, an American-born citizen, doesn't matter because we are Black. I will no longer tolerate your disdain for who we are.

I will continue to fight alongside other social justice advocates who are « good troublemakers » in the efforts to dismantle your white supremacist foundation and rebuild it to fit all of *We the People*. But in order to fight, I must first be safe, sane, and alive and so must my heir.

I have sadly found out that your white supremacy carries long, deep, global tentacles and that even when we break up with you, you can find us where we are and oppress us in a different way through different mechanisms, organizations, people, and international cooperation… but that is for another book!

We have chosen to turn all the "go back to Africa" words and looks into a powerful SANKOFA. We have taken the power out of the racist stance in those words and replaced them with "Go back and fetch it". We are going back to our roots, to fetch the spirit and might of our ancestors and to dive into that power. Nurtured in the bosom of Mama Africa, we will contribute to a global movement that values us for who we are:

Unapologetically Black, Proud, and Beautiful.

Reflection Questions

Your American dream and its shards (#mySAD)
1. What is your definition of the American Dream?
2. If you are non-white, do you feel it is fully attainable? If not, why?
3. If you are white, do you feel the opportunity to attain the American Dream is equitable among white and non-white people in the US? Why or why not?
4. What has shattered in your American Dream? Is it fixable? Do you have hope it will be? Why or why not?
5. What are three actions you feel are in your realm of power to ensure the American Dream will be alive and attainable for the next generations of non-white people in the US? Should we strive for the American Dream?

Balancing Culture (#SADculture)
1. Where do you consider your culture's origins to be? What defines your culture?
2. Have you ever been attracted to elements of other cultures? How have you dealt with that attraction?
3. How have you learned about other cultures?
4. How, if at all, have you integrated elements of another culture into your own?
5. Have there been tensions or incompatibilities and how have you dealt with those?
6. What is the value of learning about other cultures to you?
7. What are ways you might try to be more culturally competent/open?
8. What was your reaction to the concept of "ngorr"? Do you have your own interpretation of it? Share it with me on social media using **#ngorr**!

Africans, Black American and the Global Fight for Racial Equity (#SADracialequity)
1. When you think of racial equity, do you think it is an isolated problem to spaces where non-white people are minoritized? Why or why not?
2. What tensions have you seen, experienced, heard of between Africans and Black Americans?

3. If you are Black American, do you feel any connection to Africa? Why or why not?
4. If you are African, do you feel any connection to Black Americans? Why or why not?
5. How do you think racial inequity shows up in the Global Majority countries, where non-whites are the majority?
6. What do you think are the remnants of colonization in those countries and how does that perpetuate racial inequity?
7. What are some ways the Global Majority can coalesce to fight racial inequity?
8. How, if you are white, can you be a true ally to this fight with concrete antiracist action?

Being strategic and fair about migration (#SADmigration)
The issue of migration is delicate. Who owns the land we live on? If a group was already established somewhere and another arrives and takes over, how can the latter own the land and later determine its policies? Why are we still lying to children in school all over the world about Christopher Columbus "discovering" America? If a group was kidnapped and worked for free to develop a land, how can policies be maintained centuries later to ostracize them given their invaluable contribution? How can this be repaired, and the descendants of these abused groups compensated? Going back to historic migration, how do we integrate those in fairly telling the history of our world?

1. What are your views on immigration (if you are in a "developed country")? Do you see any benefits, what are they?
2. What are your views on emigration (if you are from a "developing country")? What are the benefits? What are the downsides?
3. Why do you think people leave their birthplaces to move to countries they don't know as well? Do you automatically think "to better their lives"? If so, what has influenced this automatism?
4. What do you think of the growing phenomenon of "developed country" citizens moving to "developing countries"? Why do you think they are moving?
5. How do the dynamics of emigration/immigration impact your definition of "a better life"?
6. Would you ever move to live in a different country than your own? Why or why not?

7. Have you ever pondered the treatment of "refugees" based on their places of origin (for instance Ukraine versus Sudan)? What are your observations? What could explain any differences you may see?

8. How are local policies in each country contributing to the desire for people to move? What are ways populations can advocate for policies that make their environment one they can see themselves thriving in?

9. Can you envision a world system where migration is an organized and equitable opportunity? What are some conditions you think are vital for this to become a reality?

Let's keep the conversation going (Hashtags)
I would love to hear your reflections and answers to these questions! Join the global conversation by using the hashtags dedicated to each section and share your views on one of these platforms:

Twitter (X) @rbldecolonizer

Instagram (@rebeldecolonizer)

Threads (@rebeldecolonizer)

Follow me on LinkedIn (LinkedIn.com/in/decolonizer) for more engaging conversations. To make sure I see your views and can engage with you, please always @ me on platforms with my username, and add the standard hashtags **#shatteredamericandream #antagueyejames** to your posts.

I look forward to our conversations and exchanges.

About the Author

Anta Gueye-James is a mom, public health and development professional, coach, and strategist, and forever Pan-African partisan of *good trouble*. She has spent the majority of her professional career working on social justice as a determinant of health, community development, and racial and health equity issues in the United States.

After more than twenty years studying, working, and living in the US, she decided to move her family back to the motherland in 2019 where she worked as a management executive in the International Development sector for over three years. Today, Anta is focusing on executive management coaching and youth leadership training, adding her two decades of professional experience in participation to growing the Pan-African leadership of tomorrow. She also provides strategy consulting and public speaking, while nurturing her writing, and various entrepreneurial ventures.

As a longtime lover of African arts and culture, she is committed to contributing her experience, expertise, and passion for the positive promotion, connection, and strategic development of Africa and its diaspora.

Her hope is for her next book to highlight her and others' experiences on the continent with the tentacles of white supremacy, and dive into the issues of post-colonialism society, global power imbalance, discrimination within international development, and the many shades of racism this combination produces.

Anta has always loved writing, since a very young age, and won the Lifetime TV national essay contest which accompanied the US release of the American Idol winner Fantasia Barrino's story in 2006. She also enjoys reading, traveling, culinary experiences and the arts, and often jokes that her dream job is to be paid to scour the world to eat and talk about it!

Works cited

https://www.npr.org/2019/10/02/766083651/gandhi-is-deeply-revered-but-his-attitudes-on-race-and-sex-are-under-scrutiny

https://ldhi.library.cofc.edu/exhibits/show/africanpassageslowcountryadapt/introductionatlanticworld/slaverybeforetrade

Excerpt of letter from Nzinga Mbemba to Portuguese King João III, in World History Commons, https://worldhistorycommons.org/excerpt-letter-nzinga-mbemba-portuguese-king-joao-iii [accessed January 24, 2023]

https://jikapost.com/histoire/abdoul-kader-kane-le-premier-almamy-du-fouta-toro-par-papa-gora-diop/1107/ [accessed January 15, 2023]

https://bipartisanpolicy.org/explainer/paid-family-leave-across-oecd-countries/

https://www.tomfriedenpublichealth.net

http://www.unitedwaysaskatoon.ca/me/uploads/2014/09/TheOgreStory_Branded.pdf - The Ogre Story, *A story of how short term and long term solutions must work together to create lasting change.* United Way Saskatoon & Area.

Clark, K. B., & Clark, M. P. (1947). Racial identification and preference in Negro children. In T. M. Newcomb & E. L. Hartley (Eds.), *Readings in social psychology* (pp. 602– 611). New York, NY: Holt, Rinehart & Winston

www.ingramcontent.com/pod-product-compliance
Lightning Source LLC
Chambersburg PA
CBHW030311130626
46549CB00002B/812